Basics of Islam

A Christian's Guide to Understanding Islam

By Dr. Steven A. Crane

Basics of Islam is available at special quantity discounts for bulk purchase for sales promotions, premiums, fund-raising, and educational needs.

For details write
Endurance Press, 577 N Cardigan Ave, Star ID 83669.
Visit Endurance Press' website at *www.endurancepress.com*

Basics of Islam

PUBLISHED BY ENDURANCE PRESS
577 N Cardigan Ave
Star, ID 83669 U.S.A.

ISBN 978-0-996497565

L.C.
Printed in the U.S.A.

Basics of Islam

A Christian's Guide to Understanding Islam

By Dr. Steven A. Crane

M ost Christians have a limited understanding of the Muslim faith and are ill-prepared for discussions about Islam with their friends and neighbors, not to mention discussions with other Muslims. This book is an introduction to the beliefs and principles of the Islamic faith so that we can be better prepared for dialogue with this rapidly growing religion and those who are welcoming this potentially dangerous faith into American culture.

This book is divided into two parts: understanding the tenets of Islam and, then, considering an appropriate Christian response to the Muslim on the streets of America (There are more every day!). It is my hope that this will be a useful and readable resource. For those wanting additional information, supplemental material is contained in the footnotes and in the appendices.

As motivation to my Christian friends who are reluctant to read this entire book, please consider the admonition in 2 Timothy 2:15. Here we are exhorted to:

> Do your best to present yourself to God as one approved, a worker who has no need to be ashamed, rightly handling the word of truth (ESV).

We need both the truth of His Word and the Love of His heart to successfully reach Muslims. May this book prepare you for that mission.

Contents

Appendices

Preface

Clarifications and Explanations from the Author

I must start with some words of clarification and explanation to help you understand what I am trying to accomplish and how I am going to proceed. There are four considerations that I'd like you to remember as you read this book.

First, as with Christianity, Islam has many variations. For our purposes (i.e., a concise treatment of Islam) it is necessary to make generalizations[1] and simplifications. Every effort has been made to state the standard position of Islam accurately. Understand, when you make generalizations, you will always create inaccuracies of some sort.

Second, for some, Islam is a "culture" rather than a system of faith. There are many individuals who hold to Islam as a way of life, but do not necessarily believe all that Islam teaches. This is no different than many Jews who are Jewish culturally, or even nationally, but not necessarily religiously. Nor is it far removed from the notion that America is a Christian nation—for certainly there are many who claim to be Christian, but who do not believe all the truths or

---

1 Someone once said, "Generalizations are always wrong, but usually helpful."

principles recorded for them in the Bible.[2] There will no doubt be some who will read this book and say, "I know a Muslim and they don't believe what you put forward." The simple answer is that they may not believe what is presented in this brief treatment. You should not be surprised if your Muslim friend takes a different stance on certain minor areas of theology or practice.[3] This fact, however, does not negate the core beliefs of Islam presented here.[4]

Third (and this is very significant), there is much discussion about "Radical Islam." You have been told that Islam has been hijacked by those who hold a radical view. In actuality, Islam teaches that the *Qur'an*[5] is explicit and literal, and adherents must obey the Qur'an in order to comply with Allah's[6] rules. Islam contends that all mankind should seek to know and submit to Allah's will without question or hesitation. The Qur'an requires its followers to read it literally, and a literal reading will lead one to a radical belief system. The freedom to interpret the Qur'an in a non-literal (or moderate) way is actually forbidden by the Qur'an and is not tolerated in any

2 The perception that America is a Christian nation is a major stumbling block for many Muslims. Muslims often associate Christians with American culture. To be American is to be disobedient to your elders and to dress provocatively. To be American means to act like Hollywood. To be American means smoking, drinking, cursing, wine, women, and song. They correlate being American with being Christian.

3 This is especially true with American Muslims.

4 There is also the possibility that the Muslim is invoking his Sharia "right" to not tell the truth about his faith, during a time when he is in the minority. We will address this further in our discussion of *taqiya* in Chapter Three.

5 Also spelled Koran or Quran. No system of transliteration for Arabic names is entirely satisfactory. English is simply not equipped to handle the subtleties of the Arabic alphabet accurately. Koran, Moslem, and Mohammed are older anglicized equivalents of common Arabic words. I have chosen to use Qur'an, Muslim, and Muhammed because of their more common use in English. Many other Arabic terms referenced in this work will also have possible alternative spellings.

6 Allah is the Arabic word for god. In order to avoid confusion, "Allah" will be used in reference to the Islamic god while "God" will be used for the God of Christianity.

nation under Islamic rule. Those who do hold a more "moderate" view and freely interpret the Qur'an are often themselves a target in Islamic countries because the Qur'an has explicit rules for dealing with both moderate Muslims as well as non-Muslims. Freedom of religion and freedom of interpretation do not normally exist in those countries which are under Islamic rule.[7]

Fourth and finally, I want to distinguish between Islamic ideology and Muslims as people. I do not want to berate Muslims or attack them as individuals. I want to demonstrate my love for them by reaching out to them in truth. I also want to minister to the many in our communities who have been influenced by this religion. I desire to understand this often-misrepresented religious system in the hopes of having real dialogue.

To be fair, I believe that the Islamic religion is misguided and often dangerous! My heart-felt desire is to have a positive influence upon those who are trapped within its grasp. That being said, please understand that this book is a work of love: love of the truth and love for those who have been captured by Islam. It is this same truth and love which will help Christians have a meaningful dialogue with their Muslim neighbors.

Jesus said, "If you abide in my word you are truly my disciples, and you will know the truth, and the truth will set you free" (John 8:31-32, ESV).

---

7 For a list of Islamic countries, see Appendix A.

Part One

Understanding Islamic Beliefs and Practices

One

Understanding Islam's Basic Nomenclature

I t is necessary, as we begin, to rightly define a couple of significant terms. These terms, although widely used, are often either misunderstood, glossed over, or inaccurately defined. The definitions of these terms will be discussed in further detail later, but, at this point, only foundational definitions are needed.

The Meaning of "Islam"

We have often been told that "Islam is a religion of peace," or even "Islam means peace." Both of these statements are inaccurate and misleading.[1]

Words in Arabic, as in Semitic languages in general,[2] are primarily formed from what is called a triliteral or triconsonantal root.[3] Simply put, words are based primarily on three letters or consonants.

---

1 Many American Muslims will themselves define Islam as a religion of peace and have been taught this as one of the basic principles of Islam.

2 The Semitic languages would include, but are not limited to Arabic, Aramaic, and Hebrew.

3 A root containing a sequence of three consonants.

For the purposes of our study, we can transliterate[4] the root letters of Islam as "**SLM**." The core meaning of "**SLM**" is to resign, surrender, or submit oneself. Thus, Islam (i**SL**a**M**) means: the act of submission and resignation of oneself to another (in this case, Allah). *It is not accurate to say that "Islam means peace"—it does not.*[5]

Who Is a "Muslim"?

One who professes Islam is a Muslim (mu**SL**i**M**): one who has submitted to Islam. In Islam, peace is only offered for those who have surrendered themselves to Allah. All others are to be contended against.[6]

What Is "Sharia Law"?

One of Islam's primary goals is to establish *Sharia[7] law*. This includes a mandatory and highly specific legal, social, and political plan for the whole of society. Sharia law is divided into two main sections: acts of worship and human interactions. The rules regarding worship impose disciplines on both the individual and the community; they are mandates for a life of submission to Allah. The section on human interactions includes societal rules concerning all financial transactions, endowments, inheritance, marriage, divorce, child

---

4 A process of bringing the Arabic letters into English using the closest equivalents. Since most English readers are unfamiliar with Arabic script, I have used transliteration of Arabic words throughout this book.

5 "Anyone with even the most elementary knowledge of Arabic knows that ... Islam actually means 'total surrender' or 'total submission to God.' The image the word suggests is that of a vanquished army on its knees in surrender before a victorious conqueror. The very word 'Islam' suggest the power of Allah to vanquish all opponents" (Michael Youssef, *Blindsided*, 63).

6 Islam actually requires Muslims to take revenge whenever Allah is insulted. This obviously results in conflict rather than peace.

7 Sharia means "the path." Commonly translated "Islamic law," sharia has come to signify Islam itself. Sharia is the path by which submission is enacted. It is the actual route map of religion as a way of life.

custody, penal punishments, warfare, peace and judicial matters (including the testimony of witnesses and proper forms of evidence). Let me restate this so you can capture the full force of Islamic law in the affairs of everyday life. With Sharia law, there is no separation between the religious, the social, and the political. As such, Islam is not simply "another religion" or *JUST* a religious system. Sharia law encapsulates every area of life including the organization and even the structure of society. (This is where many in our country, especially our leaders, get it wrong.)

If it does not involve the political realm, it is not Islam, because Sharia law mandates behavior at every level of life, including politics, economics, banking, business law, contract law, transactions, worship, culture, sexuality, societal interaction, social relationships, morals, behaviors, beliefs, military strategy, and governmental order. It even goes as far as mandating appropriate food and drink.[8] Every area of life, both public and private, is mandated by Sharia law. While most other legal codes deal primarily with public behavior, Sharia also includes private behavior and private belief.

Sharia law is based on the *Qur'an*,[9] *hadith*,[10] and centuries of debate and precedent of Islam. Even in areas where the Qur'an and traditions are silent, rules are derived by consensus of the religious leaders and by analogous[11] reasoning. This has led to an immensely detailed body of rules and regulations.

---

8 For example, the eating of pork is prohibited as well as the eating of any animal that was slaughtered in the name of someone other than Allah. Sharia also prohibits the eating of animals with sharp teeth, birds having claws, animals with tentacles, or eating any which did not have the blood drained completely before packaging. Intoxicants, like alcohol, are not allowed under any circumstances.

9 Islam's most holy book.

10 A hadith is an oral tradition based primarily on what Muhammed said or did.

11 To reach a conclusion by means of analogy, comparison, or similarity.

What we absolutely need to understand from the outset is that Sharia law and Western Civilization (as we know it) are incompatible. Sharia law regulates not only every aspect of life, but it also has, as its ultimate goal, the creation of an Islamic state.[12]

What Is "Creeping Sharia"?

The establishment of Sharia law in a new location is most often done through what is called *Creeping Sharia*. Creeping Sharia describes the slow, deliberate, and methodical advance of Islamic law into non-Muslim countries with the goal of making Sharia law the law of the land.

It does not take much investigation to find ongoing attempts to introduce Sharia into our country. A close look at states like Michigan and the New England States will show this process at work.[13] Watch the nightly news and you will commonly hear stories about the introduction of Islamic holidays into school calendars, discussions about Islamic garb, and even attempts to regulate court proceedings by Sharia law. This is not by accident; it is by design. If you want to get a preview of what will likely happen in the United States, look to Europe.[14] The daily conflict, the spiritual and legal warfare between Sharia law and previous law is what America will face in the next five to ten years, if Sharia is allowed to continue its usurpation of

---

12 For example, the Muslim Brotherhood's creed is "Allah is our objective. The Prophet is our leader. Qur'an is our law. Jihad is our way. Dying in the way of Allah is our highest hope."

13 Dearborn, MI, a city with a population of around 98,000 people, is roughly 30% Muslim. It contains the largest concentration of Muslims in the United States. As such, it became the first US city to officially implement Sharia Law. Do a quick internet search of Islam in Dearborn, MI to get a glimpse of this.

14 Germany, Austria, France, Denmark, Holland, the United Kingdom, and Spain (to name a few) all have Sharia courts or at least "peace judges" (judges who quote the Qur'an) which threaten the existing laws of the land.

American law.[15] The ultimate goal of Islam is to introduce full Sharia as widely as possible in the world.

---

15 Several states have already passed or are currently in the process of passing Sharia law legislation. According to BILLIONBIBLES.ORG©2016, this legislation, although seldom containing the word "Sharia," has made its way into Alabama, Arizona, Arkansas, Florida, Indiana, Iowa, Kansas, Kentucky, Louisiana, Mississippi, Missouri, Oklahoma, North and South Carolina, South Dakota, Tennessee, Texas, Virginia, Washington, and West Virginia.

two

Understanding Islam's Origins

This chapter identifies the origins and early development of Islam. The pre-Islamic age in Arabia is known as "The Period of Ignorance" (*jahiliyah*). Muslims describe this as the darkest age in human history, full of anarchy and debauchery in both the religious and social life of the world. During this period, the population in Arabia was primarily composed of scattered nomadic tribes who were largely idolatrous and polytheistic (worshiping many gods). Some sources say that the Arabs worshiped as many as 360 different deities—one for each day of the lunar calendar.

It was in this very polytheistic culture that Muhammed[1] was born (A.D. 570-632). He was born in Mecca,[2] but little else is known of his early life.[3] We do know that he was orphaned at an early age

---

1 Alternate spellings: Muhammad or Mohammed. Muhammed's full name is Muhammed Bin-Abdullah.

2 Mecca is in Saudi Arabia.

3 Scholars are unable to pinpoint many of the dates and events in the life of Muhammed exactly, and most of the facts pertaining to Muhammed's life are shrouded in uncertainty and even fantasy. One such account tells of Muhammed playing with some other children when two angels came to him and opened up his chest. The other kids were scared and thought the angels might be evil jinn and therefore, ran away. But the angels were good and took out Muhammed's heart and cleaned it until it shined. Then they put his heart back into his chest and left.

and first raised by his grandfather, and later by an uncle.

Muhammed showed great interest in religion early on, but it was not until his adult life that it took on major significance. It was while he was working as a caravan manager that he met and married a wealthy widow named Khadijah. He was 25 and she was 40. Upon marriage, Muhammed immediately became a person of importance because of her social status. Because of Khadijah's wealth, Muhammed no longer had to work and was free to take up his interest in religion.

Concerned over the polytheism in Arabia and their highly superstitious practices, Muhammed took an interest in the "One True God" of the Jews and Christians. He had heard stories about their God during his days traveling with the caravan, and this belief in a monotheistic God led Muhammed to try to unify a divided people around this concept of one God.

Humble Beginnings in Mecca

At the age of 40, Muhammed received his first revelation. After the loss of his son, he went into a cave on the slopes of Mount Hirah (approximately three miles outside of Mecca) to mourn. For some time after this loss, he would revisit the cave. During one of these visits, he went into a trance and heard voices. Interestingly enough, when he first heard voices, he attributed them to evil spirits who he thought were playing with his mind. He struggled with this for some time, but his wife Khadijah[4] eventually convinced him that he was hearing the voices of angels, not demons. Muhammed then claimed that he received revelations from God (whom he called

---

4 Khadijah had a cousin, Waraqa, who belonged to a sect of Christianity. She suggested that Muhammed might have been visited by a messenger from God.

Allah)[5] through the angel Gabriel. Then he announced that he was a prophet of Allah.

Muhammed continued to receive these "revelations" for 22 years. Considering himself to be a prophet, Muhammed began to preach and teach in Mecca.

In the early days, Muhammed went door to door trying to persuade the polytheists to abandon their idols. He invited them to accept that there was no god but Allah. His teaching was moderate, and he invited others to join him. During these early days he taught both compromise and peace, but had only a few converts.[6] Most of Muhammed's first followers were members of his own family—his wife Khadijah, his nephew Ali-ibn-Abu Talib, and Zaid, his adopted son.[7] The first adult outside the family to make a profession of Islam was Abu Bakr,[8] a wealthy merchant who became a prominent figure within Islam.

During his days in Mecca, Muhammed began to encounter fierce opposition. Some of the opposition arose from the fact that Muhammed had instructed his followers to pray towards Jerusalem—this did not sit well with the Jewish people.

Because of this conflict, Muhammed quickly changed the focal point of Islamic prayers to Mecca which became the new "Holy City."

---

5 Allah is simply the Arabic word for god and is used by Arabic-speaking Christians as well as by Muslims. But while Christians and Muslims both use the same name for God, and while they share some of the same attributes, the Christian God and Allah are not the same.

6 Most reports say that Muhammed had 15 converts in the first three years and the total number of people who fled to Medina in 622 (twelve years after his first preaching) was between 60 and 70.

7 Zaid formerly had been his slave and a gift to Muhammed from Khadijah.

8 Abu Bakr 'Abdallah bin Abi Quhafa as-Siddiq (A.D. 573-634) later became the father-in-law of Muhammed. Abu Bakr served as advisor to Muhammed during Muhammed's lifetime and became the first Muslim Caliph following Muhammed's death. Abu Bakr ruled for a little over two years before he died.

As a result, Muslims now face a holy shrine called the *Ka'ba*.[9] Other individuals and groups opposed Muhammed, accusing him of being a soothsayer and that he was demon-possessed. As the opposition intensified, Muhammed decided to leave Mecca and seek asylum in Medina.

Conquest and Power at Medina

In A.D. 622, Muhammed fled (*hijrah*) to Medina[10] where he began forming alliances with several groups of people. As a coalition, they began robbing the Meccan caravans and the booty from these raids allowed Muhammed to expand his influence. This became a turning point in Muhammed's career and it was in Medina where he began to fully develop his teachings.

There was a step-by-step progression to Muhammed's teachings. Although things started with moderation, at every stage of life his teaching became more extreme and grandiose. With the journey to Medina, Muhammed began to assert the absolute character of his revelation. He no longer made any attempt to peacefully coincide with Judaism or Christianity and he viewed his teaching as final and his revelation superior to all others. It was also during this period that daily times of prayer, ceremonial washings, and Friday as the day of worship were established.

It was also at Medina that his mission began to take on a political dimension. In A.D. 624, Muhammed fought and won the

---

9 The Ka'ba is a large cube-shaped building inside a mosque in Mecca and serves as the central shire of the Islamic religion. According to Islam, the Ka'ba was built by Abraham and his son Ishmael near the place where Ishmael and his mother Hagar wandered when they were in the desert.

10 Medina is located in Saudi Arabia. Medina means, "the prophet's own city" and contains "the prophet's mosque" which is the burial place of Muhammed. Originally called "Yathrib." It is located 250 miles north of Mecca.

decisive Battle at Badr.[11] This victory gave him great spoils and he shared the booty with those who fought with him. This battle swung Muhammed and Islam in a military direction. From this point on, war on religious grounds was sanctioned and holy war (jihad) became not only acceptable, but a religious duty for Muslims. Muhammed still sought conversion of non-Muslims. Unbelievers were still invited to submit to Allah, but now, if they refused, they were attacked. It was also at this time that Muhammed's revelations changed dramatically and Islam took on a whole new flavor at Medina.

His teaching was no longer about peace and compromise, but about conquest and power. It was at Medina that Muhammed became both a religious and a political leader. This is the reason why the A.D. 622 date is chosen to mark the beginning of the Muslim calendar,[12] which they call "year one." Don't think this point is insignificant. *The Islamic calendar starts at the moment when Islam turns from peace and compromise to conquest and power.*

It is often stated that Muhammed became popular because of his call for unity. Many claim that the movement began to grow because Muhammed was the first person who tried to unify the Arabs as one people. While it is true that Muhammed did bring

---

11 The Battle of Badr was fought on March 13, 624 in the Hejaz region of western Arabia. It was not the first battle, but it was the decisive battle that changed the course and direction of Islam. Other major battles included the Battle of Uhud (A.D. 625) and the Battle of the Trench (A.D. 627).

12 The Muslim calendar was adopted in A.D. 632. The starting point begins on July 16, 622. Years are designated "A.H." for "after hijrah." The years are purely lunar and consist of twelve months which alternate between 29 or 30 days. The Muslim year is only 354 days long. Because of the shorter calendar length, the Muslim year starts about eleven days earlier each time when compared to a typical calendar. Because of the moving calendar, Muslim months do not correspond with seasons. The names of the Islamic months are: *Muharram, Safar, Rabi al-awwal, Rabi al-thani, Jumada al-ula, Jumada al-akhirah, Rajab, Shaban, Ramadan, Shawal, Dhul qadah, Dhul hijjah.* The ninth month in each Muslim year (Ramadan) is observed as a fast. The pilgrimage to Mecca must be made in the twelfth month (*Dhul hijjah*).

various clans together, this "uniting" was not typically peaceful. In fact, little growth occurred until conquest became as important as conversion and retribution was the standard treatment for those who refused to convert.

When people refused to convert, they were attacked. If the various tribes or clans were defeated, they were given the option either to convert or die. In some instances, Jews and Christians—if they swore allegiance to Allah—could retain their faith, but only if they paid a special tax to Muhammed.[13]

Over the course of the next decade, Muhammed succeeded in creating a religious force which encompassed the economic, cultural, and political structure of the entire Arabian Peninsula. During these years, Muhammed gathered an army of 10,000 Muslim converts and marched on the city of Mecca. He seized the city and claimed it for Islam. Within the next few years, Islam had taken territory throughout the Middle East.[14] Within a century, Islam had reached across North Africa, into Europe, across Asia into China, and down into India by means of the Muslim conquests.[15]

One of the most unsettling aspects of Muhammed's life concerns

---

13 Victor Hoven writes, "Mohammed fled from Mecca to Medina in 622, which dates the beginning of the Mohammedan calendar. From this date his preaching was accompanied by the sword and the torment began. He gave people choice of one of three things—"the Koran, tribute, or the sword" (Victor Hoven, *Notes on the Revelation*, Eugene, OR: Northwest Christian College, 1949, p. 39).

14 Gibbon says that Islam "reduced to its obedience 36,000 cities or castles, destroyed 4,000 churches ... and erected 1,400 mosques for the exercise of the religion of Mohammed" (Edward Gibbon, *The History of the Decline and Fall of the Roman Empire*, Vol. 5, Chapter 50, p. 274).

15 The Muslim conquests (*al-Futuhat al-Islamiyya*) are also referred to by many as the Arab conquests because it is more politically correct. These began with Muhammed in the 7th century and continued under subsequent Rashidun and Umayyad Caliphates. The resulting empire stretched from the borders of China and India, across Central Asia, the Middle East, North Africa, Sicily, and the Iberian Peninsula, to the Pyrenees. These conquests displaced Jews and Christians and burnt down churches and synagogues, with only a few exceptions. Those churches or synagogues which were spared typically became Muslim mosques. To read more about this history, see Edward Gibbon's *The History of the Decline and Fall of the Roman Empire*.

was his use of violence to achieve his goals. Modern Muslims often claim that Muhammed killed only in self-defense, but history shows that he ordered his followers to murder people simply for writing poems that were critical of him or those who might stand in opposition to him. Apostates fared no better. Muhammed commanded, "Whoever changes his religion, kill him."[16]

Although Muhammed promoted peace and tolerance when Muslims were in the minority (Mecca), his strategy suddenly changed when his followers outnumbered his enemies (Medina). Understanding the difference between *Mecca Islam* and *Medina Islam* is one of the keys for understanding Islam today.[17] Consider three verses from the last major chapter of the Qur'an to be revealed[18] which show the radical nature of Islam after Muhammed's transition to Medina.

> Fight those who believe not in Allah nor the Last Day, nor hold that forbidden which hath been forbidden by Allah and His Messenger, nor acknowledge the Religion of Truth, from among the People of the Book, until they pay the Jizyah with willing submission, and feel themselves subdued (Surah 9:29).

> O Prophet! Strive hard against the Unbelievers and the Hypocrites and be firm against them . . . (Surah 9:73).

> O ye who believe! Fight the Unbelievers who are near to you and let them find harshness in you: and know that Allah is with those who fear Him (Surah 9:123).

---

16 Recorded in the collection of hadith compiled by Sunan An-Nasa'i, 5.37.4069. His collection is unanimously considered to be one of the six canonical collections of hadith (*Kutub as-Sittah*).

17 We will talk about these descriptions further in Chapter Three.

18 The Qur'an is not chronological. Surah 9 is the last major chapter of the Qur'an to be revealed. See Appendix B for the chronological order of the Qur'an.

Notice the radical nature of Medina Islam. The main criterion for conquest and retribution in these verses is simply that the people do not believe in Islam. Muhammed's final marching orders to his followers consisted largely of commands to violently subjugate non-Muslims. This is the nature of Islam which naturally occurs when Islam becomes prevalent.

Three

Divisions Within Islam

This chapter identifies the various divisions within Islam, focusing on the difference between Mecca Muslims and Medina Muslims. It is important to consider the various divisions that have developed within Islam. Muslims are typically categorized by two main groups (*Sunni* and *Shia*) and then further subdivided into numerous different sects—seventy-five or more.

The Sunni and Shia

The basic cause for the division between Sunni and Shia was a difference of opinion as to who should succeed Muhammed as *caliph*.[1] After Muhammed's sudden and unexpected death, his failure to appoint a successor caused great turmoil. The Sunnis (the major division of Islam) follow a line of progression through Abu Bakr, who was Muhammed's father-in-law. The Shi'ites[2] (the minority

---

1 Caliph is the Arabic word for a spiritual or political leader of a Muslim state (caliphate).

2 Adherents of Shia Islam are called Shias or the Shi'a as a collective or Shi'i individually. Shia Islam is the second-largest branch. Twelver Shia (*Ithna'ashariyyah*) is the largest branch of Shia Islam.

21

group), although they accepted the first three caliphs[3] as legitimate successors, believe that the true line of leadership of Islam continues through Ali,[4] who was Muhammed's son-in-law and cousin rather than Abu Bakr.

The Sunnis (accounting for 87 to 90 percent of Islam) are the mainline, orthodox Muslims (Osama bin Laden was a Sunni). The Shiites (about 10 to 13 percent) are often viewed as the very militant Muslims—but this is not necessarily true. Militant Muslims can be found amidst all the various sects of Islam. Various other divisions and belief systems occur within both the Sunnis and Shiites— depending greatly upon their cultural setting.[5]

Further Divisions of Islam

In addition to the two major divisions within Islam, there are many other Islamic groups and schools of thought creating other notable branches of Islam (often called sects).

The *Sufis*[6] are Muslim mystics who emphasize inner spirituality and strive for perfection of worship (*ihsan*). They are more concerned over one's inner being than over external practice. They strive to obtain a state where the soul reaches a point of absorption into god.

---

3 Abu Bakr became the first Muslim caliph following Muhammed's death. He ruled from A.D. 632 to 634. He was followed by Umar ibn Al-Khattab who became the second caliph of the Rashidun (which means "rightly guided") Caliphate and ruled from 634 to 644. Uthman ibn Affan became the third caliph of the Rashidun Caliphate and ruled from 644 to 656.

4 After the assassination of the third caliph, the Shi'ites elected Ali ibn Abi Talib to rule over their caliphate from A.D. 656 to 661. The disagreement about who should rule split the Muslim community into the Sunni and Shi'i branches. The Sunnis consider Ali the fourth and final caliph of the Rashidun Caliphate while the Shiites believe that Ali and all other Shia Imams are the rightful successors to Muhammed.

5 For example, a Muslim Sunni in East Africa is vastly different from a Muslim Sunni in Afghanistan, while a Muslim Shi'ite and a Muslim Sunni in Afghanistan are likely much closer in belief than their counterparts of either sect in East Africa.

6 Technically, Sufism is not a sect of Islam, but an esoteric, mystical movement within both Sunnism and Shi'ism.

Their goal is to "worship Allah as if you see Him; if you can't see Him, surely He sees you." Most Sufi Muslims have a spiritual guide (*murshid*) who helps them down their path to union with Allah. Their spiritual disciplines include recitations from the Qur'an, devotional prayers, breathing exercises, singing, and dancing.

The *Dervish* are the small, extreme group who swallow or walk across live coals, swallow knives and swords, and are known as the snake charmers. These practices of physical exertion (*dhikr*) are part of the process of attaining an ecstatic trance by which they reach Allah. They are also known for their extreme poverty and austerity.

Black Muslims are a group of African-American Muslims who split from the Nation of Islam in the late 1970s. They believe that white people are a hybrid race of devils. Louis Walcott (who was given the name "Farrakhan") is one of the most well known of this sect. Farrakhan continues to give voice to radical racist ideology. Other prominent Muslim groups in the Afro-American community include the Hanafi movement, the Ansaru Allah sect, and the Islamic Party of North America.

The *Bahai* faith also stems from Islam. They emphasize the spiritual unity of all humankind, suggesting not only that there is only one god, but that all major religions have the same spiritual source and come from the same god. They teach that god has sent to humanity a series of divine Educators known as "Manifestations of God." The primary purpose of these educators is to advance civilization. They consider Abraham, Krishna, Zoroaster, Moses, Buddha, Jesus, and Muhammed to be among those Educators. The Bahai faith today is guided by a governing council called the Universal House of Justice.

In addition to these sects there are many other divisions as well: *Shafi, Malaki, Wahabi, Salafists, Hanbali, Barelvi, Deobandi, Zaidi, Ismali, Twelvers, Ibadi, Kharijite,* etc.

A Better Categorization of Islam

For the purposes of this book, and to gain a better understanding of world events, there is actually a better and more accurate way of dividing Islam. Rather than dividing Islam into the conventional categories, Sunni, Shia, and other branches; Islam can, and should be, divided into two major categories based on the nature of their observances. A more helpful division of Islam would then be MEDINA MUSLIMS and MECCA MUSLIMS.[7] It should also be noted that these are not my categories. These categories are recognized within Islam itself.

Medina Muslims

This group is the most problematic. Medina Muslims are the fundamentalists of Islam (of all sects) who live by the strict letter of their creed and follow the teachings of Muhammed after his theology had fully developed in Medina. They require rigorous adherence to Sharia law and make it a requirement of faith that Sharia be followed by everyone. These are the Muslims who are often referred to as radical or even *Millenarian Muslims*. The Medina Muslims attempt to institute Sharia by force—they see this as their religious duty. Medina Muslims most often call Jews and Christians "pigs and monkeys." Medina Muslims prescribe beheading for the crime of "nonbelief" in Islam. Medina Muslims practice stoning for adultery and hanging for homosexuality. Medina Muslims put women in burqas[8] and beat them if they leave their homes alone. Medina Muslims murder infidels. They preach *jihad* and glorify death as godly, revered martyrdom. They make it a crime

---

7 See earlier discussion in Chapter Two about what Muhammed taught and how Muhammed acted in Mecca as opposed to Medina.

8 Transliterated burkha, bourkha, or burka. It is an enveloping outer garment used to cover a woman's body in public. The face-veiling portion is called a hijab.

for nonbelief. This viewpoint comes from a rigid adherence to a literal reading of the Qur'an and is prevalent in those nations where Islam is the predominant religion. In fact, there is no Muslim majority nation that allows for a non-literal reading of the Qur'an. Majority Muslim nations, for the most part, are dominated by Medina Muslims.[9]

Mecca Muslims

Mecca Muslims consist of Muslims who are loyal to the core creed of Islam and worship devoutly, but do not overtly practice violence. They base their faith and practice on the early revelations given to Muhammed while in Mecca. They attend religious services and abide by the religious rules prescribed by Islam, but live in an uneasy tension between belief and culture. Mecca Muslims are those who are often associated with peace and compromise and are sometimes referred to as moderate Muslims.[10]

In Muslim-majority countries, Mecca Muslims are themselves often a target of Medina Muslims because they do not follow a fundamental, literal understanding of the Qur'an.

In Muslim-minority countries, Mecca Muslims try to balance the observance of their faith within the constraints of a different culture. This conflict between faith and culture is especially evident in Western settings. Some Mecca Muslims are able to resolve this tension, while many others are able to cope only by withdrawing into a very sheltered environment through a process called "cocooning."

---

9 A few majority Muslim countries have tried being Muslim secular states. Jordan, Egypt, and Turkey have been the noteworthy examples in the past. Egypt, however, has since been overtaken by the Islamic brotherhood, and the 2016 revolts in Turkey had at their core the move away from being an Islamic secular state as their President Recep Tayyid Erdogan pushed it once again toward religious rule.

10 Are there moderate Muslims? If by "moderate" we mean less zealous and less extreme, then there are certainly moderate Muslims. For more information, see the questions asked in Chapter Seventeen.

Cocooning

All Muslims (Medina or Mecca) who live in countries where Western values are practiced, live in what is best described as a state of cognitive dissonance—they are trapped between Islamic belief and Western culture. They live in a daily struggle to adhere to the teachings and practice of Islam while at the same time struggle to live in community. Often, they will withdraw from public life if at all possible. Cocooning is a practice where Muslims attempt to wall off outside influences and live privately by their religious beliefs. They frequently permit (or certainly prefer) only an Islamic education for their children, commonly dress entirely in Islamic garb, and often disengage from the wider community in which they live. This practice of cocooning obviously limits assimilation into different cultures.

In actuality, there are only two alternatives for all Muslims who want to practice Islam while at the same time trying to live within Western culture: leave Islam, or reject the culture of the West and practice a lifestyle of cocooning.[11] In truth, the hope of nearly all Muslims is to bring Islam (and specifically Sharia law) to the mainstream in order to be able to practice the tenets of Islam openly and publicly.

Taqiya

One of the most troubling aspects of Islam is the practice of *taqiya*.[12] This doctrine was first developed for dealing with situations of religious persecution where Muslims could save their lives by concealing their true beliefs.[13] It was later extended to allow deception in order

---

11 The practice of cocooning makes assimilation into Western culture nearly impossible.

12 Also spelled *taqiyya* or *taqiyyah*. Taqiya is lying to advance the cause of Islam and/or prevent harm to Muslims. It literally means "prevention."

13 Muslims justify taqiya from Surah 3:28 and from other Islamic texts. For example: *The*

to advance the cause of Islam. In modern practice, Islam allows its followers to lie and deceive and even deny Islam—as long as they continue to adhere to belief in their hearts. Many hadiths speak to this practice and suggest that lying is permitted in the following situations: in war and espionage; to bring reconciliation between two parties who have quarreled; and to deceive a nonbeliever.[14] *Taqiya today is considered appropriate if it helps someone or advances the cause of Islam.*

Taqiya is routinely practiced in areas where Islam is not prevalent. One specific area that taqiya can be seen is through a Muslim's pretended friendship with a non-Muslim, because the Qur'an forbids real friendship with infidels.

Let not the believers Take for friends or helpers Unbelievers rather than believers: if any do that, in nothing will there be help from Allah: except by way of precaution, that ye may Guard yourselves from them. But Allah cautions you (To remember) Himself; for the final goal is to Allah (Surah 3:28).

Taqiya is encouraged in order to conceal the true beliefs of Islam in non-Islamic areas. When pressed, Muslims have actually admitted this. "We have one vocabulary in private and we have another vocabulary for the public domain and that's why you don't hear it because you are in the public domain."[15]

Taqiya takes many other forms as well.

- There are English translations of the Qur'an that are specifically designed to appeal to Westerners and to dispel all of the fears and anxieties about Islam. These translations,

Life of Muhammed by Ibn Ishaq, p. 307.

14 According to the Qur'an, Allah himself often misleads and deceives people to advance his own cause.

15 Dr. Patrick Sookhdeo, *Islam and Truth*, Barnabas Fund, 2007.

done under the tenets of Taqiya, wander greatly from the original texts and from normal Islamic interpretation.[16]

- Taqiya is also seen in the practice of disseminating false "facts" to elevate the status of Islam. This is occurring on college campuses and universities, as well as through the media. The purpose is to make Islam appear in a better light, covering up the negative realities of Islam.[17]

- Taqiya is used in making peace treaties with non-Muslims when it is advantageous for the Muslims. When circumstances change, however, so that it becomes advantageous for the Muslims to break the treaty, they must do so.

The first duty is to firmly believe in their invalidity and that because they contain invalid conditions they were born dead the very day they were given birth to . . . The second duty of the Muslim is to believe that these treaties do not bind him and that it is not lawful for him to give effect to any of their contents except under compulsion and necessity . . . The third duty is to work towards overthrowing these treaties.[18]

Abrogation

As stated earlier, while there are many varied divisions within Islam, the most useful classification is to place followers of Islam into the categories of MECCA MUSLIMS or MEDINA MUSLIMS.[19] This type

---

16 Ibid.

17 For examples of this, see Appendix E.

18 'Abdul Rahman 'Abdul Khaliq. Islamic scholar from Saudi Arabia as quoted in *Islam and Truth*, Barnabas Fund, 2007.

19 Some, acknowledging that the verses revealed to Muhammed in Medina are significantly more militant and violent than the verses he received in Mecca, prefer to use the classifications of "strong" verses and "weak" verses. In either case, "strong" verses supercede, abrogate, and cancel out the earlier "weak" verses of the Qur'an.

of classification requires that a person clearly grasp the principle of *abrogation*,[20] the reality of taqiya, and understand the differences in the teaching of Muhammed in his early years in Mecca, and his later teachings in Medina.[21]

At a minimum, the principle of abrogation states that later revelations (either by divine declaration of Allah or by precedent of the prophet Muhammed) make null and void the earlier pronouncements. This requires that the principles of jihad and conquest nullify the previous principles of peace and compromise, because the later revelations abrogate the earlier ones. In this case, a fundamental form of Islam lays claim to being the true observance of Islam because it is following the later pronouncement of Muhammed, and moderate Muslims are not practicing Islam appropriately because they are following revelation that has been abrogated.

At a much deeper level, however, the Muslim application of the principle of abrogation actually prescribes a different set of instructions to its adherents depending on the relative prominence of Islam. This understanding is much more instructive as it confirms and validates the behaviors and beliefs of both the moderate Muslims in the West and the radical Muslims elsewhere. In predominantly Muslim nations, we can see the Medina principles in full force—radical Islam governed by Sharia law with its violent tendencies. In the United States (and other Western cultures), where Islam has not yet taken root, Mecca Muslims give the appearance of peace and compromise, and may through taqiya, even deny the radical nature of Islam. According to this deeper understanding, once Islam gains numbers and status, we can expect that the Medina principles will emerge even in the West.

---

20 Abrogate means to repeal or cancel by authority. The principle of abrogation will be talked about later, but is a key principle in Islam.

21 These issues will be brought up again throughout the pages of this book.

I believe you can see the evidence of this in places like Dearborn, Michigan and in some of the New England states already. This is certainly being borne out already in European nations.

Four

The Importance of Studying Islam

The importance of studying Islam is demonstrated by the fact that there are now over one and a half billion[1] followers of Islam around the world (Islam now counts among its adherents one out of every four people on earth). The importance of studying this issue is intensified when you realize that Islam is now the fastest-growing religion in the world. It is rapidly expanding through converts, conquest, and conception.

Conception may, now, have surpassed all other factors in Islam's growth. According to the Pew Research Center, Muslim majority communities have an average population growth rate of 1.8% per year. This compares with a world population growth rate of 1.1% per year and a population growth rate in the United States of 0.7% per year.[2] It is predicted that the world's Muslim population will grow

---

1 1,570,000,000.

2 This population growth rate is only made possible by the number of legal and illegal

twice as fast as non-Muslim populations over the next 20 years. If these trends continue, it is predicted that within the next 50-75 years, 35% of the world's population will be Muslim.

Islam is a driving force behind over fifty nations in the Middle East, Africa, and Asia.[3] More than thirty-five countries now have populations that are over ninety percent Muslim. Islam is now the second-largest religion in Europe and the third-largest in the United States.[4] There are now between five and seven million Muslims in America—a number that is up nearly two million in just the last couple of years.[5] The states of Michigan, New Jersey, and Massachusetts contain the largest Muslim population centers in America, and many states (especially in the West)[6] are accepting thousands of Muslim refugees.

Unlike many religions, Islamic leaders aggressively pursue a mission to affect not only religious beliefs, but social, political, economic, and military arenas as well. The principal goal of Islam is to bring Islamic law (Sharia law) to every nation. This includes a mandatory and highly specific legal, social, and political plan for the whole of society. There is no separation between the religious, the social, and the political. As such, it is not simply "another religion," or "just a religious system." As stated previously,[7] Sharia law

immigrants entering the United States, many of which come from Muslim nations.

3 See Appendix A for a complete listing of these countries.

4 According to a 2014 study by Pew Research Center the rankings would be as follows: *Christianity, Judaism, and Islam. *This categorization lumps all various Christian groups into one, including Protestant, Catholic, and various other groups which claim to be Christian.

5 Estimating Muslim population growth is a contentious political issue. Many Islamic organizations have accused American demographers of releasing falsely low population numbers of Muslims in the United States to justify the marginalization of Muslims.

6 My own state of Idaho is among those receiving a large number of immigrants and refugees. Kuna, Idaho and Twin Falls, Idaho rank among the highest.

7 See Chapter One.

addresses every aspect of culture, including the organization and structure of society. If it does not involve the political realm—it is not Islam—because Sharia law specifies mandatory behavior in every aspect of life including worship, culture, societal interaction, transactions, contracts, morals, behaviors, beliefs, punishments, and governmental order. All areas of life are mandated by Sharia, and religion and politics are the two sides of a single coin in Islam.

Sharia Law

Islamic law, called Sharia law, is the religious legal system governing the members of the Islamic faith. Most Muslims hold that Sharia protects them from sin and serves as an identity marker separating them from non-Muslims.

Surprisingly, there is great diversity in Islam regarding Sharia law and the average Muslim (especially in the West) is not well versed in its various requirements. It is derived primarily from the Qur'an and the Hadith (the sayings and life example of Muhammed), but is also based on centuries of debate and precedents of Islam and Islamic scholars.

Sharia law sets itself up as the law of Allah in direct opposition to human legislation. According to Islam, *Sharia law abrogates all other law and demands that ruling power be given to Muslims.*[8] Sharia law specifically defines crime, the judicial process, justice, and the punishments given for the violation of Sharia law. These are often in direct violation with the existing law of non-Islamic countries, and certainly in direct contradiction with the Constitution of the United States and our system of jurisprudence. Sharia law defines criminal law, civil law, constitutional law, contractual law, inheritance law,

---

8 Under Sharia, Jews and Christians (*dhimmi*) are to be treated as a conquered and subjugated people. They are considered second-class citizens and must adhere to a number of restrictions designed to reinforce this second-class status.

personal affairs, and even marriage and divorce law. Sharia law also defines the punishments and punitive damages that are required for the breaking of Sharia.[9]

What many (especially among our political leaders) fail to realize is that Sharia law and the laws governing the United States of America are incompatible. Sharia law contradicts and nullifies our form of government, cultural mores and values, human rights, and even freedom of thought. And yet, surveys show that the vast majority of Muslims in the United States desire to be governed by Sharia.

Muzammil H. Siddiqi, who was invited by President George W. Bush to lead a prayer at the Washington National Cathedral a few days after 9/11, clearly proclaimed this agenda when he wrote:

> Allah's rules are not limited to the acts of worship, they also include social, economic and political matters. By participating in a non-Islamic system, one cannot rule by that which Allah has commanded . . . As Muslims we should participate in the system to safeguard our interest and try to bring gradual change . . . *We must not forget that Allah's rules have to be established in all lands*, and all our efforts should lead to that direction.[10]

According to Islam, Sharia law supercedes all other law, and all Muslims are to work towards the establishment of Sharia law. In fact, *Muslims who deny the validity of Sharia or criticize it in any way are labeled as non-Muslims (infidels or apostates) and face the threat of being treated as such.*

With Sharia law there is no freedom of speech, there is no freedom of religion, there is no freedom of artistic expression, there are no equal rights, and there is no democracy. With Sharia

---

9 Punishment for crimes under Sharia often include such penalties as amputation for theft, stoning for adultery, and religious killings for those who are apostates to Islam.

10 "Apologists or Extremists: Muzammil Siddiqi," Investigate Project on Terrorism, April 20, 2011, www.investigativeproject.org/profile/171. Italics mine.

law there are certainly no women's rights, nor is there the freedom to bear arms (unless you are Muslim). Ultimately, under Sharia law, there are only three options available for "non-Muslims" (conversion to the Muslim faith, suffer high taxes, or persecution and even death).

Examples in Europe

As mentioned previously, if you want a preview of where we are headed in America, take a look at Europe today. The actions by Muslims in Europe are based on Sharia law. Let me list just a few examples.

- In the streets of London, there are times when traffic cannot move because Muslims are found praying in the streets.

- Entire areas of Europe are considered no-go zones for non-Muslims. This includes the police.

- In parts of Europe, Christians may not speak to Muslims about Christianity, nor may Christians hand out literature. This law is being enforced by British Courts.

- In some areas of Europe, during Ramadan, non-Muslims cannot eat or drink where a Muslim can see them.

Examples in America

And Sharia is finding its way to America. Examples include:

- Within the United States of America, many schools are making classrooms available for Islamic prayer and school calendars often include Muslim religious holidays.

- In some settings, head scarfs are being allowed in situations where head-coverings were previously forbidden (i.e., for driver's license pictures, and legal I.D. cards).

- In many school districts, textbooks are being vetted by Muslim organizations before they are used in public schools.

- In some school districts, students practice calligraphy by writing the Muslim statement of faith, "There is no god by Allah. Muhammed is the messenger of Allah."[11]

- In various states, court cases have been allowed to appeal to Sharia law in order to reach a verdict.

- In mid-November 2006, Minnesota Congressman Keith Ellison was sworn into office with his hand upon the Qur'an.[12]

- In early September 2016, President Barack Obama nominated Muslim Judge Abid Riaz Quereshi to fill a seat on the U.S. District Court for the District of Columbia. If confirmed, Qureshi would be the first-ever Muslim federal judge.

- Maybe the clearest example of Sharia law finding its way to America happened on December 10, 2015. On that Thursday, Carolyn Walker, who was also hand-picked by President Barack Obama, was sworn in as judge of the 7th Municipal District Court of Brooklyn, New York. She was

Judge Carolyn Walker sworn in while holding a copy of the Qur'an.

11 School districts in Virginia were reported doing this in December of 2015.

12 As of the writing of this book, Keith Ellison is being considered to chair the Democratic National Convention.

sworn in using the Qur'an. The most glaring problem with this precedent for swearing in a judge is that the Qur'an forbids all law but Sharia law.

With the rapid growth of Islam, and the over-reaching scope of political correctness, it is imperative that we take measures not only to understand what is happening, but to prevent the continued deterioration of our American, Judeo-Christian culture. More importantly, it is necessary for Christians to be equipped to reach this rapidly expanding people group for Christ.

Five

The Qur'an and the Hadith

I slam's teaching is based primarily on the Qur'an and the Hadith.

The Qur'an

The Qur'an[1] is the central religious text and sacred book of Islam. "Qur'an" is derived from the Arabic word *qara* which literally means "recital" or "recitation." Muslims believe the Qur'an to have been verbally revealed by Allah to Muhammed through the angel Gabriel over a period of about twenty-three years.[2] For the Muslim, the Qur'an is the word of Allah in the most literal sense and takes precedence over all other religious books. Muhammed was merely the recipient of the word and passed along Allah's word. Nabeel Qureshi explains how special the Qur'an is to the Muslim:

---

1 Alternate spellings: Quran, Koran.

2 The revelations to Muhammed began on December 22, 609 (when Muhammed was 40) and continued until his death in 632.

Muslims believe that every single word of the Quran was dictated verbatim by Allah, through the Archangel Gabriel, to Muhammed. The Quran is therefore not only inspired at the level of meaning but at the deeper level of the words themselves. For this reason, Muslims do not consider the Quran translatable. If it is rendered in any language other than Arabic, it is not Quran but rather an interpretation of the Quran. A book can be a true Quran only if written in Arabic.[3]

Islam teaches that the Qur'an bears no marks of Muhammed's character and Muslims consider it blasphemous to attribute to Muhammed a single verse—even in a secondary sense.

The Gathering of the Qur'an

According to tradition, Muhammed did not write down the revelations as he received them,[4] but taught these revelations orally to his students. After his death, several of Muhammed's pupils, who had memorized parts of that teaching, began to preserve his teaching by writing down his words. These were not written down immediately,[5] nor were they recorded by any one individual, which resulted in many varied and contradictory collections of Muhammed's revelations.[6]

The first caliph, Abu Bakr, instructed an aide named Zayd,[7]

---

3 Nabeel Qureshi, *Seeking Allah, Finding Jesus*, 37/346 digital version.

4 Most believe that Muhammed could neither read nor write, though there are some who debate this point.

5 Arabic writing was far from perfected during the time of Muhammed and there were no written Arabic books at that time. Later, when writing the text of the Qur'an began, letters and vowel markings were still being standardized, which led much to confusion and variation.

6 While many Islamic scholars have attempted to argue this point, modern scholarship has shown definitively that there was no complete set of collated and arranged revelations at Muhammed's death or even in the immediate years following.

7 Zayd ibn Harithah was a companion of Muhammed and regarded as his adopted son. He is the only companion whose name appears in the Qur'an, Surah 33:37.

to gather and assemble the text from a variety of sources.[8] These compilations had so many differences that the third caliph, Caliph Uthman ibn Affan, later tried to establish a standard version now known as Uthman's codex which is the basis of the most widely circulated version of the Qur'an. He created a somewhat standardized text between A.D. 650 and 656, which he circulated widely. He then ordered that all other versions be condemned and burned in A.D. 657. Variants, however, continued to exist well into the tenth century when some Islamic scholars were imprisoned for refusing to abandon their preferred versions. Even until the mid-twentieth century, two versions were still in use with one version held widely in most Islamic countries and another version being used in North Africa. There are also various other texts called "readers." These will be dealt with later in this book.

The Arrangement of the Qur'an

Next to the Bible, the Qur'an is the most-read book in the world. It is approximately the same size as the New Testament, but is very different in scope, style, and content. The Qur'an contains mostly poetry. Most Muslims love the Qur'an, not for what it says (many cannot read),[9] but how it sounds when it is read.[10] It is not chronological, biographical, or philosophical. It is not even arranged by

---

8 Most Muslims mistakenly believe that the Qur'an was completed during Muhammed's lifetime, or that it was at least completed by Abu Bakr. This is easily demonstrated to be inaccurate.

9 This is true even for Arabic speakers. Arabs speak and write colloquial forms of Arabic that vary by region. Qur'anic Arabic is often much different than what they know. The language of Islam is personal only to a very few.

10 The fact that Muslims believe the words themselves are "perfect" leads many Muslims to neglect the meaning of the words—it is enough just to say the words. Using the exact word is more pious than understanding the meaning of the words. There are many who can recite chapter upon chapter of the Qur'an from memory but cannot explain the meaning or the context of those verses.

themes or doctrines, but primarily according to the length of the passages.

In some cases there are no divisions or sections within the text. While most modern versions do give the text different sections, some do not number either verses or paragraphs. Among those texts which do give numbered divisions, there still remains some divergence. Where the text is divided, the chapters are called surahs and the verses are called *ayahs* or *ayats*—meaning "signs." The standard arrangement in the more modern versions is 114 chapters. There is also an inconsistency between English and Arabic versions.

The surahs (chapters) are arranged according to length: the longest at the beginning, the shortest at the end.[11] Due to this arrangement, many of the earliest surahs are found at the end of the Qur'an.[12] This arrangement also means that verses that were uttered years or decades apart are frequently found side by side with no obvious connection, while verses uttered in the same context are separated within the Qur'an. The surahs are often given a heading consisting of a word or two, the meaning of which can be a theme in that chapter.[13] Many surahs also include a notation to indicate the place of revelations, whether Mecca or Medina.[14] Some Muslims also

---

11 The first surah is the exception. It is a short prayer addressed to Allah which Muslims recite daily. The rest are messages from Allah to his people and are arranged in descending order of length, with Surah 2 being the longest.

12 I have provided a chronological listing of the surahs in the Qur'an in Appendix B at the back of the book.

13 Some of the chapter names include: The Cow, The Bee, The Ant, The Moon, The Victory, The Disbelievers, etc.

14 It should be noted that earlier surahs evidence more tolerance toward Christians and Jews while later surahs reflect the rejection of those same people groups. The last major surah given was Surah 9 which reads, "Fight and slay the Pagans wherever you find them" (9:5) and "Fight the unbelievers who are near you (9:123). Remember, according to the Qur'an itself, later revelations abrogate the earlier revelations (see Surah 2:106 and 16:101).

divide the Qur'an into thirty parts so that the Qur'an can be easily recited during the thirty days of Ramadan.

The Content of the Qur'an

The content of the Qur'an can be easily categorized into three groups: regulations which govern the Islamic community, warnings about the coming judgment, and stories about the various prophets. Other than information about Allah, there is little information about other doctrinal issues such as creation, paradise, hell, or other matters of theology.

Claims for the Qur'an

Muslims believe the Qur'an to be the infallible word of Allah.[15] They claim that the Bible has been tampered with, and that the Qur'an corrects the inappropriate changes to the Bible. They believe that the Qur'an is written in the "living" language of Arabic, which means that it can still be understood, and is therefore more reliable. They believe that the Qur'an is eternally pre-existent[16] and that it super-cedes all previous revelations (including itself). Although direct contradictions exist in the Qur'an, they are not viewed as problems, but are viewed through a lens of abrogation.[17]

The Hadith

In Islamic terminology, a *hadith* is a saying, narrative, or report from the life of the prophet Muhammed. Hadiths are second only to the Qur'an in importance in Islam. As was the case with the Qur'an, the individual sayings of Muhammed were not written down imme-

---

15 This topic will be discussed in much more detail later in this work.

16 There is some debate in Islamic circles on this issue.

17 Abrogation states that later pronouncements nullify earlier ones. This will be explained later in this chapter.

diately by Muhammed, nor by any other scribe. Hadith literature is based on spoken reports that were circulated after the death of Muhammed and were evaluated and gathered into different collections. They contain statements or actions of Muhammed and often cite his approval or disapproval of events that happened in his presence. The collected traditions of the hadith cover all sorts of subjects: moral teaching, religious duty, legal problems, and various theological themes.

Each hadith contains two parts. The first part contains the actual narrative of the saying or event. The second part describes the chain of transmission by which the report was handed down. Islamic scholars spend a great deal of time and effort debating whether a particular hadith is "strong" or "weak." Their determination, however, does not affect their belief in its truthfulness.

Almost three decades after Muhammed's death, Caliph Uthman ibn Affan (a successor of Muhammed) began to collect and arrange the various hadiths. That process continued over the next two generations (8th and 9th centuries) as large collections were compiled. Because these accounts were not written down immediately, nor were they written down by just one person, many different hadiths exist. So many variations were collected, that a specific text was never agreed upon. Today there remain many variations. Six great collections of Muslim tradition exist.[18] The numerous variations are not just translation differences, but often contain wording that is completely opposite in meaning. What is puzzling to many of us Westerners is that opposite wording is deemed equally binding.[19]

---

18 The Al-Kutub Al-Sittah (the authentic six) are formed by the following collections: Sahih Bukhari (collected by Imam Bukhari), Sahih Muslim (collected by Muslim b. al-Hajjaj), Sunan al-Nasa'i (collected by al-Nasa'i), Sunan Abu Dawood (collected by Abu Dawood), Jami al-Tirmidha (collected by al-Tirmidhi), and Sunan ibn Majah (collected by Ibn Majah).

19 Once again, much clarity is brought to the issue by understanding Mecca and Medina

Translation

Islam teaches that all languages except Arabic are inferior[20] and therefore, no translation of the Qur'an is accepted as binding. In reciting the Qur'an, Islam teaches that the words themselves are miraculous and unreproducible and so the Qur'an should only be recited in Qur'anic Arabic.[21] Almost all translations of the Qur'an will carry the description of "a translation" or even the phrase "an interpretation," which signifies that the translated work is not official or binding. In quoting both the Qur'an, and the Hadith, it is essential that you quote the particular version you are using to avoid confusion.

Abrogation

Unlike the Bible,[22] Islam has "a doctrine of abrogation" (naskh) in regards to the Qur'an and the Hadith. Abrogation is a process of reconciling contradictory material within a primary source of Islam. Simply put, not all verses in the Qur'an or the Hadith have the same weight in veracity.

A common explanation for dealing with contradictions states that later pronouncements of the Prophet override earlier pronouncements. In fact, the Qur'an itself gives this explanation:

> None of Our revelations do We abrogate or cause to be forgotten, but We substitute something better or similar: knowest thou not that Allah hath power over all things (Qur'an 2:106).[23]

Muslims.

20 Speakers of Arabic have a special prestige in the eyes of the Muslim world.

21 Also called classical Arabic.

22 Some might argue that the Bible also has a doctrine of abrogation—suggesting, for example, that the New Testament abrogates the Old Testament. Jesus, however, said, "Do not think that I have come to abolish the Law or the Prophets; I have not come to abolish them but to fulfill them" (Matthew 5:17, ESV).

23 *An English Translation of the Holy Qur'an*, by Abdullah Yusuf Ali. Chapter and verse

When We substitute one revelation for another,—and, Allah knows best what He reveals (in stages),—they say, 'Thou art but a forger' but most of them know not (Qur'an 16:101).

Allah doth blot out or confirm what He pleaseth: with Him is the Mother of the Book . . . (Qur'an 13:39).

If it were Our Will, We could take away that which We have sent thee by inspiration: then wouldst thou find none to plead thy affair in that matter as against Us (Qur'an 17:86).

This being the case, it is important to understand that many of the teachings of Islam have been abrogated and are not to be given the same weight or are not to be followed at all.[24] It becomes imperative then to remember that the Qur'an is not chronological. Many of the oldest surahs are placed at the end of the Qur'an, and some of the most recent are near the beginning. It is not that those at the end of the Qur'an abrogate the ones listed earlier, but that the ones revealed later, abrogate the earlier ones—regardless of where they are found in the Qur'an.[25]

As mentioned earlier, both the Qur'an and Hadith contain numerous variations. These are not just translation differences. Sometimes the verses contain wording that is completely opposite in meaning, or at least wording that changes meaning significantly. These opposing verses, however, are not seen as contradictory. Actually, many of them are viewed as different sets of instructions to be carried out depending on whether: an area has established a

---

numbers in the Qur'an, and its various English translations are not standardized. But the passages quoted can usually be found within a verse or two of the numbers given in various translations.

24 As long as a Muslim knows the relative dates of two contradictory verses, they can tell which one to ignore (the early one) and which one to obey (the later one).

25 I have supplied a chronological listing of the surahs in the Qur'an in Appendix B.

caliphate or not, is under Sharia law or not, or whether Islam is in a position of prominence or not. A position of prominence is not necessarily a "majority" but often happens when it reaches approximately sixteen percent of the population (remember Creeping Sharia?).[26] Many Islamic scholars divide the Qur'an and Hadith into two parts: verses revealed by Muhammed when his community of followers was weak (in Mecca where the people were taught to compromise and live at peace), and verses revealed where Muhammed was strong (in Medina where revelations took on another character altogether).

Therefore, many Islamic scholars maintain that there are verses that are to be obeyed when a country is under a caliphate,[27] and other verses to be followed while Islam is in the minority. In other words, there are Medina verses and Mecca verses. Stated differently, some passages apply when Islam is the predominant religion of the land, and some passages apply when Islam is NOT predominant. This should help us understand why Islam takes on a more radical nature when a country is predominantly Muslim and why countries where the Muslim population is increasing are experiencing pockets of unrest.

At the risk of being redundant, let me state the principle of abrogation again. At a minimum, abrogation declares that later pronouncements declare null and void earlier pronouncements. This being the case, it is paramount to understand when each surah was given.[28] More specifically, many Islamic scholars divide the Qur'an into Mecca verses and Medina verses. *Mecca verses are to be applied*

---

26 We will talk more about this when discussing "Migration as Jihad" (*Al-hijra*) in Chapter Seven.

27 A caliphate is a Muslim area deemed to be ruled by a Muslim leader (caliph) with the Qur'an as its only constitution.

28 A chronological listing of the surahs is given in Appendix B.

when Islam is NOT dominant in the region while Medina verses are to be applied when Islam IS dominant.

Islam now has a field of Qur'anic exegesis called "the abrogator and the abrogated" in which they determine the criteria and history of when and how to apply the principle of abrogation. Many Muslim scholars list up to five hundred verses of the Qur'an which fall into the category of abrogated texts.

Six

Islamic Beliefs

The religion of Islam consists of two parts: Belief (*iman*) and Practice (*din*). In this chapter we will focus on Islamic beliefs and in the following chapter Islamic practices.

Core Beliefs

All Muslims are bound by a single creed based on the Qur'an called *The Shahada*.[1] This core creed binds all Islam together regardless of their sectarian differences. This creed, revealed by the angel Gabriel to the Prophet Muhammed, unites all Muslims. All Muslims, without exception, know the words of Shahada by heart. The Shahada goes as follows: "I bear witness that there is no god but Allah; and Muhammed is His prophet/messenger."

Regardless of sect or geographical setting, generally Islamic groups all have four core threads that tie them together: (1) their respect for the Qur'an; (2) their respect for Muhammed; (3) their emphasis on the Arabic tongue; and, (4) their hatred for Western culture (America—the great Satan in particular) as demonstrated

---

1 Shahada means: to observe, to witness, to testify.

by their strict adherence to a Middle-east mentality.[2]

All Muslims must accept the following six basic beliefs, or articles of Islamic Faith: Faith in Allah, Angels, the Holy Books, the Prophets, Predestination, and the Day of Judgment.

Faith in Allah (*tawhid*)

Muslims believe there is only one true god and that his name is Allah. His will is supreme. As part of their daily life, they must constantly "confess" him with their tongue to show belief of their heart.

The full confession, called the shahada, is as follows:

"I believe in Allah, his angels, his books, his prophets, in the last day, in the predestination by the Most High Allah of good and evil, and in the resurrection after death."

A briefer summary is, "I testify that there is no Allah but Allah and I testify that Muhammed is the Apostle of Allah."

Muslims lay tremendous emphasis on the unity, majesty, transcendence and sovereignty of Allah. He has no partner nor children. According to Islamic doctrine, the power and immutability of Allah make him the author of all things: all things good AND bad.

To deny Allah is called *shirk*[3] and it is the worst of sins. The most common shirk is giving to Allah "an equal." The Christian "trinity"[4] is considered by Muslims to be shirk—the greatest of all sins. In many Muslim countries, committing a shirk is punishable by death.

---

2 Islamic society demands strict conformity of its members—it is the thinking of the group, particularly the family, that matters most. In Islamic nations, all Muslims follow the prescribed rules. Because of this, most Muslims fail to distinguish between the Christian faith and Western culture. They think of America as a Christian nation and then look to Hollywood and conclude that movies and TV depict acceptable behavior to Christians. They abhor the low standards of public morality among the people and identify it with Christians.

3 Shirk means association.

4 Most Muslims believe that Christianity is polytheistic—worshiping three gods. It is important to point out that Christianity is monotheistic—worshiping one God in three persons. We will talk more about this later in Chapter Thirteen.

Angels (*malaikah*)

Muslims believe in a hierarchy of angels, who are reasoning created beings who were made out of light. While they are reasoning beings, they do not have free will and must serve Allah. They were given special functions by Allah. They watch over humans and record their deeds. The greatest angel is Gabriel (*Jibrail*) who transmitted the Qur'an to Muhammed. Gabriel is also referred to as the Holy Spirit (*Rul ul'Amin*).[5] Other angels include Michael (*Mikail*),[6] Israfil (*Israfil*),[7] and Israel (*Izrail*).[8]

In addition, Muslims believe that every person is assigned two angels who are responsible for recording the individual actions of that person. One angel records sins, while the other records good deeds.

Muslims also believe in the *jinn*, who were created from smokeless fire. The jinn are like demons and because they do have freewill some are good and beneficent, but typically the jinn are bad. These shadowy spirits inhabit ruined houses, desert places, and mountain canyons. Many Muslims live in dread of evil jinn and take precautions to protect themselves from an attack.

The devil (*Iblis*) or Satan (*Shaytan*), is sometimes described as an angel, but normally as a jinn. Iblis is often referred to as the father of all jinn.

The Holy Books (*kutub*)

Muslims believe that Allah has given a long series of revelations (104 books), including the Old and New Testaments. The first hundred

---

5 Gabriel strengthened Jesus so that he could perform his prophetic duties.

6 Michael is called the provider.

7 Israfil is the trumpeter of doom.

8 Israel is the custodian who has the care of the faithful at death.

books have been lost and only four of these remain: The Books of Moses (*Tawrat*, Torah/Pentateuch); The Book of David (*Zabur*, the Psalms); The Books of Jesus (*Injil*, the Gospels, or for some, the New Testament in general); and The Book of Muhammed (Qur'an). The supposedly lost books[9] include teachings that were given to Adam, Noah, Abraham, and other prophets.

It is claimed that the Jews and Christians changed and distorted their own Scriptures, so Allah sent the Qur'an to correct the problems. The Qur'an is the final (as well as pre-existent and eternal) revelation to mankind and supersedes and essentially abrogates the others. It is the most perfect revelation of Allah. The fact that Muslims consider the Qur'an to be perfect is puzzling to Westerners because of the fact that it abrogates[10] and contradicts itself.

The Prophets (*nabi*)

Muslims believe Allah has sent numerous prophets to mankind. According to the traditions there have been 124,000 prophets.[11] The Qur'an gives the names of 28 prophets—most of whom are biblical characters.[12] A Muslim will not deny any of the prophets of the Old Testament, and will acknowledge John the Baptist and Jesus in the New Testament (Surah 2:285).

Nine are regarded as major prophets: Noah, Abraham, David, Jacob, Joseph, Job, Moses, Jesus, and Muhammed. The six principal

---

9 Although Muslims claim there are books that have been lost, there are no historical records that even suggest this.

10 To repeal by authority. See "abrogation" in Chapter Five.

11 It is important to note that the word "prophet" in Islam does not mean the same thing that it does in the Bible. The Qur'an uses the term to mean a divinely appointed leader (one who has submitted), not necessarily one who prophesies. Prophets in Islam have a higher status than all other people.

12 The list of Islamic prophets includes many who are not mentioned in the Bible, nor are mentioned anywhere else outside of the Qur'an.

prophets are Adam—the chosen of Allah, Noah—the preacher of Allah, Abraham—the friend of Allah, Moses—the speaker of Allah, Jesus—the word of Allah, and Muhammed—the apostle of Allah. Of all the prophets, only Jesus is perfect, only Jesus is in heaven, only Jesus will return. The recognition of these prophets by Islam serve as good witnessing points.[13]

Because Muhammed's revelation is considered the greatest of all, he is called the "Seal of the Prophets" and "Peace of the World" among 200 other titles given to him. Other titles include: the messenger, the beloved, the chosen one, the trustworthy, the honest, the truthful, the kind, the perfect, the witness, the announcer, the noble, the shrouded, the generous, the eraser, the opener, the gatherer, and the holy one.[14]

Muslims also believe that Muhammed is predicted by the New Testament in passages which refer to the *paraclete*—the Greek word for comforter (i.e., The Holy Spirit).

Muslims do not worship Muhammed, or any of the prophets, but consider them godly examples. None of the prophets (including Jesus or Muhammed) are considered divine.

Predestination (*wa al-qadr*)

Muslims believe that everything that happens (both good and evil) have been predestined by Allah's will, which is his immutable decree. Muslims are told to submit unconditionally to Allah's will. A key phrase is: "*Maktub, Maqdur, Kismat*"—"It is written, it is decided, it is my lot." Allah has measured out the span of every person's life—their lot of good or ill fortune, and the fruits of their efforts.

---

13 We will discuss this topic in Chapter Fourteen.

14 All of the various names given to the prophet Muhammed are easily found by doing a quick search on the internet.

The Day of Judgment (*mi'ad*)

On the Last Day or Day of Judgment, Jesus will return as a Muslim.[15] All humanity will be raised again to life and will wander about for forty years during which time the books containing the record of their deeds will be examined. Each person will be judged according to his own book of deeds which have all his words and actions recorded. All deeds will be weighed on a scale—one side hanging over paradise and the other over hell.

> Then those whose balance (of good deeds) is heavy—they will attain salvation. But those whose balance is light, will be those who have lost their souls; in Hell will they abide (Surah 23:102-103).

Then everyone will have to cross a very narrow bridge called a *sirat*. Some Muslims will be saved immediately, some will fall off the bridge into hell and afterwards be released. The non-believers[16] will all fall into hell and remain there forever. While good deeds are necessary for a person to obtain salvation, ultimately that decision is only made by Allah's immutable decree regardless of one's good deeds. For most, therefore, there is no assurance of salvation.

---

15 It is important to remember that Muhammed is dead, but Jesus is alive in heaven until his return on the Day of Judgment.

16 Called infidels.

Seven

Islamic Practice

I n addition to the core religious beliefs discussed in the previous chapter, Islam also requires strict adherence to several fundamental practices.

Required Religious Duties

Every Muslim must practice at least five fundamental religious duties called the Pillars of Islam.[1] They are: reciting the creed of Islam, prayer, observing the month of fasting, giving alms to the poor, and pilgrimage to Mecca.

Reciting the Creed of Islam

Recitation of the shahada[2] is the most common statement of faith for a Muslim. A Muslim must repeatedly recite the shahada throughout the day, "There is no god but Allah and Muhammed is his prophet."

---

1 Also called Pillars of Religion (*arkan-ud-din*). In addition to the Five Pillars, Muslims are expected to "commend good and reprimand evil" and they are forbidden to gamble, charge interest on loans to fellow Muslims, or to consume alcohol or pork. Some Muslims also consider jihad to be a religious duty.

2 Shahada means: to observe, to witness, to testify.

This statement is whispered by Muslim fathers into the ear of their newborn children as well as into the ear of a dying person. It is a mandatory part of each of the five daily prayers. The shahada is also the formal process by which a person becomes a Muslim.

Prayer

A call to prayer (*adhan*) is issued five times daily and must be done in Arabic. I have included the transliteration of the Arabic call to prayer so you can get a feeling for the repetitive nature of these rituals. The following is the daily call to prayer (translations are in parenthesis):

Allahu Akbar, Allahu Akbar, Allahu Akbar, Allahu Akbar ("Allah is the Greatest," repeated four times).

Ashhadu al la ilaha illa-llah. Ashhadu al la ilaha illa-llah ("I bear witness that nothing deserves to be worshiped except Allah," repeated twice).

Ashhadu anna Muhammadar Rasulu-Ilah, Ashhadu anna Muhammadar Rasulu-Ilah ("I bear witness that Muhammed is the Messenger of Allah," repeated twice).

Hayya 'ala-s-sala, Hayya 'ala-s-sala ("Come to prayer," repeated twice, turning the face to the right).

Hayya 'ala-l-falah, Hayya 'ala-l-falah ("Come to success," repeated twice, turning the face to the left).

Allahu Akbar, Allahu Akbar ("Allah is the Greatest," repeated twice).

La illaha illa-llah ("Nothing deserves to be worshiped except Allah").

The call to prayer is sounded by a Muslim crier (*muezzin*)[3] from a tower called a *minaret*. This is part of the Muslim public place of worship called the *mosque*.

In response to the call to prayer, Muslims are to complete the prescribed ceremonial washings called *wudhu* or purification. The process goes as follows: the hands are cleansed by washing them up to the wrists; the mouth is cleansed by means of a toothbrush or simply rinsing with water; the nose is cleansed within the nostrils with water; the face is washed; the right arm, and after that, the left arm is washed up to the elbow; the head is wiped over with wet hands—the three fingers between the little finger and the thumb of both hands being joined together; and then the feet are washed up to the ankles, first the right and then the left.

After their cleansing rituals they face Mecca[4] to pray and follow prescribed postures[5] and repeat precisely worded prayers in Arabic. Since the postures and words are memorized, and most do not know Qur'anic Arabic, there is nothing extemporaneous or personal about the prayers—for most Muslims, these prayers are simply rote repetition; their daily duty.

There are longer and shorter standard prayers. The following is a translation of part of the longer prayer which is to be recited in Qur'anic Arabic.

> Surely I have turned myself, being upright wholly to Him who originated the heavens and the earth and *I am not of the polytheists.* Surely my prayer and my sacrifice and my life and my

---

3 A muezzin is the person appointed at a mosque to lead and recite the call to prayer.

4 In the West, you might even find a Muslim pull out a compass to find the right direction. One can even buy prayer rugs that have a compass built right into the rug itself.

5 At each prayer, they must adopt a routine of physical posture: standing, kneeling, bowing, and falling prostrate with their hands and face to the ground (and so on).

death are for Allah, the Lord of the worlds, no associate has He; and this I am commanded and I am one of those who submit. O Allah! Thou art the King, none is to be served but Thee; Thou art my Lord and I am Thy servant . . .

Prayers are done at the prescribed times: dawn (fajr); noon, soon after mid-day (dhuhr); mid-afternoon ('asr); soon after sunset (maghrib); and after nightfall (isha).[6]

A special Friday (jumaa)[7] prayer is required on the Muslim holy day and takes the place of the customary mid-day prayer. It is preceded by an address (khutba) and is delivered by the imam[8] or caliph.[9]

Fasting

There are three types of fasting (sawm) recognized by the Qur'an. There is ritual fasting, fasting as compensation for repentance, and ascetic fasting. Only the first, and most common, will be discussed here.

Ritual fasting is obligatory in Islam. Muslims observe a month of fasting called "Ramadan."[10] This fast commemorates the first revelation of the Qur'an that Muhammed received in A.D. 610. The

---

6 The prayer times normally become a schedule for Muslims, waking up in time for fajr, taking a morning break from work for zuhr, going home after asr, having dinner after maghrib, and preparing for bed after isha.

7 Jumaa means "congregated," and can be prayed only with three or more people present.

8 An imam is an Islamic leadership position. It is most commonly used in the context of worship—as the prayer leader in the mosque. Shi'ites believe this to be a divinely appointed position.

9 A caliph is a person considered a religious successor to the Islamic prophet and a leader of the entire Muslim community. The Sunni branch of Islam believes that the caliph should be elected by Muslims or their representatives. The Shia branch believes that a caliph is chosen by God and must be a direct descendant of the line of Muhammed.

10 Ramadan is regarded as one of the Five Pillars of Islam. The month lasts 29-30 days based on the visual sightings of the crescent moon.

fast is obligatory during the ninth month of the Muslim lunar year. The time changes each year according to the lunar calendar and can take place during any season of the year: Spring, Summer, Winter, or Fall. The fast, which includes abstinence from food, also includes abstinence from smoking and marital relations. The fast takes place from dawn to sunset and thus the hours devoted to the observance of Ramadan vary greatly depending on the season in which it occurs. Although Muslims are required to fast during the day, eating is permitted at night.[11]

Only young children and the mentally disabled are excused. The sick, the traveling, pregnant women, etc., may postpone it to another time. In some Islamic countries, there are fines that can be levied against anyone who does not participate in Ramadan.

Almsgiving

There is also a mandate on giving which is often referred to as "giving alms to the poor" (*zakah* or *zakat*). It is the religious duty of all Muslims to share two-and-a-half (2.5%) percent of their income and pay two-and-a-half (2.5%) percent on all their belongings through a very complicated system. For non-Muslims in Muslim countries, the rate of taxation is often much heavier (reaching 20% or more). It is a form of required religious tax exacted on all Muslims and on all forms of their wealth. Notice that it is involuntary and thus is not like Christian charity. It differs in several other ways as well. These alms are not used for the poor (even though they are so named) but are only distributed among certain categories or groups who have been deemed "entitled" to receive it.[12]

---

11 The irony of fasting at Ramadan is that many Muslims gain weight during this 30 day period.

12 In some Islamic nations (and in some radical mosques in the United States) an approved purpose of these alms has been to fund jihad activities and to furnish supplies for Islamic

There are other various types of voluntary alms that are given over and above the mandatory required alms.

Pilgrimage to Mecca

Every Muslim who is physically and financially capable must make a pilgrimage to Muhammed's place of birth. This is required at least once during the lifetime of every Muslim and there are many prescribed conditions that must be met: a pilgrim cannot borrow money to take the trip; it must be taken during the twelfth month (*Dhul hijjah*); the pilgrims dress in white; and, they must touch their hand (or an object which must touch their hand) to "the Ka'ba."[13] When the pilgrim touches the stone he must say:

> O Allah, I do this in Thy belief and in verification of Thy book and in the pursuance of Thy prophet's example. May Allah bless and preserve him! O accept Thou my supplication, diminish my obstacles, pity my humiliation, and graciously grant me Thy pardon.

Other responsibilities of the pilgrimage include visiting the sacred well of Zamzam, camping for eight days in the desert, and a final ritual called the "Stoning and the Feast of Sacrifice." Islamic tradition says that Abraham brought Ishmael (not Isaac) into the desert to sacrifice him but Satan intervened and Ishmael stoned him. Pilgrims re-enact this by throwing 49 stones at three "Satans" made of stone.

One of the greatest honors a Muslim can claim is to have made the pilgrimage. Those men who have done so are qualified to wear

---

terrorists. In October 2001, the United States Treasury Department froze assets of numerous Muslim organizations believed to have been specifically linked to the al-Qaeda terrorists. Other Islamic organizations within the US have been shown to be engaged in collecting and dispersing money to support jihad activities such as Hamas, Islamic Jihad, Hezbollah, and al-Qaeda.

13 The Ka'ba is a black stone which Muhammed said fell from heaven. He claimed it was once white, but the sins of man turned it black.

the white cap and add *al-Hajj* to their names signifying their having participated in the pilgrimage.[14]

Jihad

It is worth mentioning that some Muslims regard jihad (often translated as "holy war") as a sixth pillar of Islam.[15] The word jihad literally means "exertion." It is often described as an internal (spiritual) struggle to a Western audience[16] but it almost always refers to an external (defending Islam) struggle.[17] Islam allows no permanent peaceful coexistence with infidels. Jihad is the required duty of Muslims to go to war to defend Islam against perceived enemies. Anyone who dies bravely in a holy war is deeply honored and guaranteed rewards in paradise. Jihadists are considered martyrs for Islam.[18] Being a martyr, for some, may be the only way to gain assurance of eternal life. For others, pilgrimage to Mecca carries equal weight.

---

14 There are some Muslims who believe that the pilgrimage to Mecca will give assurance of salvation, although this remains a minority view.

15 Jihad will be discussed in more detail later in this work.

16 Attempts to define jihad as an internal struggle are only found in curriculum designed for Western audiences. Because early Muslim history is so full of instructions on warfare, it is pointless to present jihad as anything less than military fighting in Arabic regions. See David Cook, *Understanding Jihad*, p. 43.

17 It has been shown that ninety-seven percent of all references to jihad in the Qur'an and the Hadith refer specifically to warlike jihad against unbelievers. Only three percent can be interpreted to refer to jihad as an inward spiritually struggle. (Brad Hughes, *American Thinker*, July 16, 2011, www.americanthinker.com/2011/07/the_worldview_war.html.)

18 Many Mecca Muslims consider external jihad (fighting for Islam) obligatory. We will cover jihad in Chapter Eight.

Eight

The Theology of Islam

Concerning God

Islam teaches that the true god is the Muslim deity, Allah. They lay tremendous emphasis on the unity, majesty, transcendence and sovereignty of Allah. He has no partner or children. All other views of god (especially the Jewish and Christian God) are false.

> Allah! There is no god but He,-the Living, the Self-Subsisting, Eternal (Surah 2:55; 3:2).

> There is no god but Allah and Muhammed is his prophet (Shahada).

Islam claims it is false to assert the Doctrine of the Trinity. Thus Christians are considered unbelievers because they accept this doctrine.[1]

> They do blaspheme who say: Allah is one of three in a Trinity: for there is no god except One Allah. If they desist not from their

---

1 See Matthew 28:19; John 1:1, 14; Acts 5:3-4.

word (of blasphemy), verily a grievous penalty will befall the blasphemers among them (Surah 5:73).

O People of the Book! Commit no excesses in your religion: Nor say of Allah aught but the truth. Christ Jesus the son of Mary was (no more than) a messenger of Allah, and His Word, which He bestowed on Mary, and a spirit proceeding from Him: so believe in Allah and His messengers. Say not "Trinity": desist: it will be better for you: for Allah is one Allah: Glory be to Him: (far exalted is He) above having a son. To Him belong all things in the heavens and on earth. And enough is Allah as a Disposer of affairs (Surah 4:171).

According to Islamic doctrine, the power and immutability of Allah make him the author of all things, whether they are good or bad.[2]

Concerning the Character of God

Allah has a different nature and character than the God of the Bible. It is interesting that the list of the "99 beautiful names for Allah," which Muslims memorize and use for worship, does not contain the word "love."[3] While Allah is described as loving those who do good deeds, he is not categorized as "love," but is primarily a god of transcendence and power.

Names for Allah include the absolute ruler, the pure one, the guardian, the compeller, the controller, the supreme, the evolver, the bestower, the restrainer, the subduer, the constrictor, the abaser, the humiliator, the judge, the accounter, the sublime, the bringer of judgment, the forceful one, the watchful, the bringer of death, the perceiver, the determiner, and the avenger.[4]

---

2 God is even called the great deceiver. See Surah 3:26; 4:88; 14:4; 17:97; 74:31; 74:55-56.

3 The Qur'an records twenty-four times that Allah has no love for the sinner.

4 A complete list of the 99 names of Allah is easily found by doing an internet search. Wikipedia gives these names by searching: The Names of Allah in Islam.

Concerning the "Knowability" of God

Allah is ultimately unknowable and incomprehensible. For this reason, Allah as a personal father is repugnant to Muslims and is seen as blasphemous. One Muslim author writes:

> Allah is the unique, unexplorable, and inexplicable one—the remote, vast, and unknown god. Everything we think about him is incomplete, if not wrong. Allah cannot be comprehended.[5]
>
> We humans can never know Allah . . . People cannot know Allah and should not even try to know him. Allah is not involved in the affairs of humans . . . The Christian claim that humans can have a relationship with God is a . . . metaphysical impossibility.[6]

Concerning Jesus

Islam praises Jesus as a prophet of Allah and will often even acknowledge Jesus to be a sinless person—which is interesting, because they don't claim this of Muhammed. But Islam believes that Jesus was merely one of Allah's many prophets or messengers.

> Certainly they disbelieve who say: "Allah is Christ the son of Mary" . . . Whoever joins other gods with Allah,—Allah will forbid him the Garden, and the Fire will be his abode. There will for the wrong-doers be no one to help. They disbelieve who say: Allah is one of three (in a Trinity:) for there is no god except one God. If they desist not from their word (of blasphemy), verily a grievous chastisement will befall the disbelievers among them . . . Christ the son of Mary was no more than a Messenger; many were the Messengers that passed away before him . . . Say: "O People of the Book! Exceed not in your religion the bounds (of what is proper), trespassing beyond the truth, nor follow the

---

5 Abd-al-Masih, *Who is Allah in Islam?*, 36.

6 George Houssney, "What Is Allah Like?" Quoted from Reach Out, vol. 6, p. 12.

vain desires of people who went wrong in times gone by,—who misled many, and strayed (themselves) from the even Way" (Surah 5:72-77).

He was no more than a servant: We granted Our favor to him, and We made him an example (Surah 43:59).

Although accepting Jesus' miraculous virgin birth, Muslims deny that he was God, God's Son, or God in the flesh because that would make Allah divisible—more than one. It is a sin to claim that Jesus is the Son of God or to suggest the idea of the Trinity. Actually, when it comes to the Trinity, Muhammed had the mistaken view that the Godhead of Christianity was composed of God, Mary, and Jesus. He further suggested that Christians believe that God had sexual relations with Mary and from this union produced Jesus.

And behold! Allah will say: "O Jesus the son of Mary! Didst thou say unto men, worship me and my mother as gods in derogation of Allah'?" He will say: "Glory to Thee! never could I say what I had no right (to say). Had I said such a thing, thou wouldst indeed have known it. Thou knowest what is in my heart, Thou I know not what is in Thine. For Thou knowest in full all that is hidden" (Surah 5:116).

The Christian view of Jesus Christ as God's Son is considered blasphemous to the Muslim.

O People of the Book! Commit no excesses in your religion: nor say of Allah aught but the truth. Christ Jesus the son of Mary was (no more than) a Messenger of Allah, and His Word, which He bestowed on Mary, and a Spirit proceeding from Him: so believe in Allah and His Messengers. Say not 'Three:" Desist: it will be better for you: for Allah is One God: glory be to Him: (far Exalted is He) above having a son. To Him belong all things in the heavens and on earth. And enough is Allah as a Disposer of affairs (Surah 4:171).

Further, that He may warn those (also) who say, "Allah hath begotten a son:" No knowledge have they of such a thing, nor had their fathers. It is a grievous thing that issues from their mouths as a saying. What they say is nothing but a falsehood (Surah 18:4-5).

They disbelieved indeed those that say that Allah is Christ the son of Mary (Surah 5:17).

Any person who believes that Jesus Christ is God has committed an unforgivable sin called shirk—the association of another god with Allah. It is a sin that will send a person to hell forever.[7]

Concerning the Holy Spirit

Muslims deny that there is such a being as the Holy Spirit. Again, Allah is indivisible and there can be no other gods beside Him. Islam believes that the Godhead (or Trinity) is totally erroneous and a blasphemy because this doctrine places other beings equal with or beside Allah. Muslims believe that passages in the Bible that refer to the Holy Spirit are in reference to the angel Gabriel or even to Muhammed himself.

Concerning Salvation and Forgiveness

Islam teaches that the true religion of Allah is Islam. Salvation is available only through the teachings of Allah. Salvation requires a person to be a member of the Islamic faith.

If anyone desires a religion other than Islam (submission to Allah), never will it be accepted of him; and in the Hereafter he will be ranked of those who have lost (Surah 3:85).

Those who reject Faith. And die rejecting,—on them is Allah's curse, and the curse of angels, and of all mankind; They will

---

7 See Surah 5:72.

abide therein: their penalty will not be lightened, nor will respite be their (lot) (Surah 2:160-161).

Forgiveness is conditioned upon good works and Allah's predetermined choice. By striving to please Allah by good works (personal merit), they strive to gain Allah's favor.

> One Day every soul will come up struggling for itself, and every soul will be recompensed (fully) for all its actions, and none will be unjustly dealt with (Surah 16:111).

> Allah loveth those who make themselves pure (Surah 9:108).

"Works" are weighed on a scale with good works being heavy and bad works being light.

> But those whose balance is light, will be those who have lost their souls, in Hell will they abide. The Fire will burn their faces, and they will therein grin, with their lips displaced (Surah 23:103-104).

Even with "good works" the Muslim is not assured of salvation. You can only do two things to possibly improve your chances. First, you must accept Allah and his prophet Muhammed. Second, you can do good works and everything that is required by Allah (i.e., the pillars of religion, make a pilgrimage to Mecca, participate in jihad). But ultimately, only being predestined to heaven by Allah's favor will ultimately matter.

In Islam, there is no atonement for sin. Allah simply chooses who he wants.

> Lo! Allah forgiveth not that a partner should be ascribed unto Him. He forgiveth (all) save that to whom He will. Whoso ascribeth partners to Allah, he hath indeed invented a tremendous sin (Surah 4:48).

The day it arrives, no soul shall speak except by His leave: of those (gathered) some will be wretched and some will be blessed. Those who are wretched shall be in the Fire: There will be for them therein (nothing but) the heaving of sighs and sobs: They will dwell therein for all the time that the heavens and the earth endure, except as thy Lord willeth: for thy Lord is the (sure) accomplisher of what He planneth. And those who are blessed shall be in the Garden: They will dwell therein for all the time that the heavens and the earth endure, except as thy Lord willeth: a gift without break (Surah 11:105-108).

Concerning Jesus' Crucifixion and Resurrection

Islam teaches that Jesus Christ was neither crucified nor resurrected; therefore, it is impossible that salvation can be had through faith in Christ. For a Muslim, it is unthinkable that God would permit one of His prophets to be crucified.

That they said (in boast), "We killed Christ Jesus the son of Mary, the Messenger of Allah";- but they killed him not, nor crucified him, but so it was made to appear to them, and those who differ therein are full of doubts, with no (certain) knowledge, but only conjecture to follow, for of a surety they killed him not (Surah 4:157).

Muslims believe that Allah substituted someone else on the cross in Jesus' place. Most believe it was Judas who died. They cannot accept the fact that a great prophet such as Jesus could ever be permitted to die in such a terrible way. Muhammed believed that if Allah could not protect His prophet Jesus from a cruel death, then Allah would have failed. If Jesus did not die on the cross, he obviously did not raise from the dead. Only good works, abstention from wickedness and Allah's favor can save a man.

Concerning Fatalism

In Islam, everything is fatalistic.[8] The Qur'an teaches that everything that has been created is controlled by a fixed decree. "Indeed, all things were created with predestination" (Surah 54:46).

Muslims believe that everything that happens (both good and evil) have been predestined by Allah's will, which is his immutable decree. Muslims are told to submit unconditionally to Allah's will. A key phrase is: "*Maktub, Maqdur, Kismat*"—"It is written, it is decided, it is my lot." Allah has measured out the span of every person's life—their lot of good or ill fortune, and the fruits of their efforts.

In addition, the Qur'an teaches that Allah not only chooses some to be saved, but also chooses those who will be condemned.

> Now Allah leaves straying those whom He pleases and guides whom He pleases: and He is Exalted in power, full of Wisdom (Surah 14:4).

Concerning Jihad

There appears to be only one way a Muslim can gain assurance of his salvation—jihad.[9] But what appears at one point to guarantee salvation, certainty is unclear elsewhere. While vague at places, most Muslims do adhere to this guarantee of paradise by participating in jihad. If any guarantee of salvation is possible, it is only available through valiant death in battle.[10]

> And if ye are slain, or die, in the way of Allah, forgiveness and mercy from Allah are far better than all they could amass (Surah 3:157).

---

8 See discussion on predestination in Chapter Six.

9 See the Appendix C on jihad to find additional references from the Qur'an on this topic.

10 Some Muslims would place the pilgrimage on an equal footing.

Therefore, when ye meet the Unbelievers (in fight), smite at their necks; At length, when ye have thoroughly subdued them, bind a bond firmly (on them): thereafter (is the time for) either generosity or ransom: Until the war lays down its burdens. Thus (are ye commanded): but if it had been Allah's Will, He could certainly have exacted retribution from them (Himself); but (He lets you fight) in order to test you, some with others. But those who are slain in the Way of Allah,- He will never let their deeds be lost. Soon will He guide them and improve their condition, And admit them to the Garden which He has announced for them (Surah 47:4-6).

Jihad is often defined as war with non-Muslims. (Non-believers are enemies of Islam.)

For the unbelievers are your sworn enemies . . . Seek out your enemies relentlessly . . . You shall not plead for traitors . . . Allah does not love the treacherous or the sinful (Surah 4:101-104).

Jihad is conditional upon bravery of the individual and ultimately—God's favor.

O ye who believe! when ye meet the Unbelievers in hostile array, never turn your backs to them. If any do turn his back to them on such a day - unless it be in a stratagem of war, or to retreat to a troop (of his own)—he draws on himself the wrath of Allah, and his abode is Hell,—an evil refuge (indeed)! It is not ye who slew them; it was Allah: when thou threwest (a handful of dust), it was not thy act, but Allah's: in order that He might test the Believers by a gracious trial from Himself: for Allah is He Who heareth and knoweth (all things). That, and also because Allah is He Who makes feeble the plans and stratagem of the Unbelievers (Surah 8:15-18).

Immigration as Jihad (*Al-Hijra*)

Migration is so important that the Islamic calendar is based upon the Hijra—Muhammed's migration from Mecca to Medina. It is important to ask why the calendar is set at the point of Muhammed's migration. Why not set the calendar from the birth of Muhammed, or even the date of his first revelation? The answer is found in the fact that it was not until Muhammed moved to Medina that Islam began to have any success. It is in Medina that Islam began to take root and jihad developed.

So important is the migration of Muhammed, that Islam teaches that those who immigrate to a foreign country for the purpose of implementing Islam and Sharia receive the same reward in heaven as those who fight for Islam by the sword.[11] Such tactics can be seen in the demographic changes that we have seen in Europe over the past decades and are beginning to see in the United States. This has troubling implications when it comes to the issue of refugees from Syria and elsewhere.

The first step of Al-Hijra is for Muslims to enter a country and then demand certain religious privileges be afforded them. This is often a fairly easy process as politically correct and tolerant societies are more than happy to comply with their religious demands. As this happens, slowly other demands are made, usually in regards to school activities, Islamic holidays, Islamic dress, court proceedings, and considerations for times of prayer in the work place environment. As long as the Muslim population remains under two-percent (2%) in any given country, Muslims tend to be regarded as a peace-loving minority and are not seen as a threat to other citizens. This is the case, for the most part, in: The United States (1%), Australia (1.5%), Canada (1.9%), China (1.8%), Italy (1.5%), and Norway (1.8%).

As Islam reaches about two percent (2%) of the population, Muslims begin to proselytize from other ethnic minorities and dis-

---

11 The practice of immigration for the purpose of implementing Sharia law is called by some "stealth jihad."

affected groups. This is clearly seen in countries where Islam has exceeded the two-percent threshold, as well as within individual communities where Islam has taken root—even if the country itself has not reached this level. Here are some countries where Islam has exceeded the two-percent threshold and this practice is clearly seen at work: Denmark (2%), Germany (3.7%), The United Kingdom (2.7%), Spain (4%), and Thailand (4.6%).

At a level of about five-percent (5%) of the population, Muslims begin to exercise an inordinate amount of influence (in proportion to their percentage of the population) on society. For example, they will demand the introduction of *halal* food (clean or permissible by Islamic standards), increase pressure on government agencies to recognize Islamic customs and practices, and an increased lobbying for changes in legislation. This is rapidly occurring in: France (8%), the Philippines (5%), Sweden (5%), Switzerland (4.3%), the Netherlands (5.5%), and Trinidad & Tobago (5.8%).

At this point, and beyond, there will be increased pressure by the Islamic community to get the ruling government to allow them to rule themselves under Sharia law—which is the ultimate goal of Islam.

As the Muslim population increases, any opposition to Islam will result in uprisings and threats. This has clearly been demonstrated to be true, even as tensions have been raised due to cartoons about the prophet Muhammed, or films which were critical to Islam.

After reaching approximately sixteen percent (16%) of the population, nations begin to change rapidly and can expect large sections of society to be ruled by Sharia law.

It is important to understand that in some countries where Islam remains well below the percentages described, there are Islamic pockets of higher Muslim populations where these activities are already occurring—even within the United States.

Nine

The Qur'an Compared to the Bible

The Qur'an is the jewel of Islam. Muslims regard the Qur'an more highly than any other physical object in the world. Muslims believe that the Qur'an is perfect and without error,[1] but that the Bible is not accurate. It is common to hear something along these lines:

> Every single word, every single letter, every single stroke of the Qur'an remains exactly as it was revealed, from Allah down to Muhammed down to our day.[2]

While Muslims believe that the teachings of the Qur'an are in harmony with the original autographs of the Bible, they also believe that the Bible has been corrupted through the years so that the ones currently in use by Christians are unreliable.

The Qur'an is the only book ever to withstand the microscopic

---

1 Surah 10:37-38; 17:88.

2 Qurenshi, Nabell. *No God But One*, 272.

and telescopic scrutiny of one and all, without the book stumbling anywhere.[3]

Certainly, anyone who examines both the Qur'an and the Bible must admit that, as they now stand, they contradict one another significantly. There are major distinctions as to: the nature of God, the nature of Jesus, the means and method of salvation, the nature of mankind, and even Scripture itself.

Differences Between the Qur'an and the Bible

Notice a few of the historical differences between some of the teachings of the Qur'an and the Bible.

- The Qur'an teaches that Noah's ark came to rest on top of Mt. Judi while the Bible says it was Mt. Ararat.

- The Qur'an teaches that Abraham's father was Azar while the Bible says his name was Terah.

- The Qur'an states that Abraham attempted to sacrifice his son Ishmael while the Bible says it was Isaac.

- Muslims believe that Noah's flood occurred in Moses' day while the Bible says the flood occurred long before Abraham, Isaac, Jacob, and Joseph—and certainly before Moses led the children of Israel out of Egypt.

- The Qur'an teaches that Mary gave birth to Jesus under a palm tree rather than in a manger.

- The Qur'an teaches that Abraham was a Muslim and that the disciples of Jesus were first called Muslims, not Christians.

- The Qur'an teaches that Jesus is merely a prophet while the Bible teaches that Jesus is the Son of God.

---

3 Musa Qutub and M. Vazir Ali, *The Holy Qur'an: Arabic Text, English Translation and Commentary*, 1032)

Other differences include the belief that the Gospels often speak of Muhammed rather than Jesus and that the Jews returned to Egypt after the Exodus. You can also find alternate creation accounts and literally hundreds of other differences between the Qur'an and the Bible. [4]

Contradictions in the Qur'an

Not only does the Qur'an contradict the Bible, it contradicts itself. The Qur'an teaches that one of Noah's sons didn't go into the ark, and thus was drowned in the Flood.

> And Noah called out to his son, who had separated himself (from the rest): 'O my son! Embark with us, and be not with the Unbelievers!' The son replied: 'I will betake myself to some mountain; it will save me from the water.' Noah said: 'This day nothing can save, from the Command of Allah, any but those on whom He hath mercy!'—and the waves came between them, and *the son was among those who were drowned* (Surah 11:41-42).

But the Qur'an also teaches that all of Noah's family were saved from the flood.

> (Remember) Noah, when he cried (to Us) aforetime: We listened to his (prayer) *and delivered him and all his family* from great distress. We helped him against people who rejected Our Signs: truly they were a people given to Evil: so We drowned them (in the Flood) all together (Surah 21:76-77).

This is only one example of many internal contradictions in the Qur'an of which there are hundreds. Here are a few more examples. [5]

- Can Allah be seen (did Muhammed see his Lord)? Yes (Surah 53:1-18; 81:15-29), No (Surah 6:102-103; 42:51).

---

4 For many more examples see www.answering-islam.org.

5 For many more examples see www.answering-islam.org.

- Should Muslims show kindness to their parents? The Qur'an commands all Muslims to show kindness to their parents, even if they are not believers (Surah 17:23-24; 31:14-15; 29:8), but demands that they not show any love or friendship to those who oppose Muhammed even if they are their own parents (Surah 9:23; 58:22).

- Which was created first? The heavens (Surah 79:27-30) or the earth (Surah 2:29)?

- What was man created from? A blood clot (Surah 96:1-2)? Water (Surah 21:30; 24:45; 25:54)? Burned clay (Surah 15:26)? Dust (Surah 3:59; 30:20; 35:11)? Or a drop of thickened fluid (Surah 16:4: 75:37)?

- Where did calamity come from? From Satan (Surah 38:41)? From Ourselves (4:79)? Or From Allah (4:78)?

- Does Allah command to do evil? No (Surah 7:28; 16:90). Yes (Surah 17:16).

- Can Allah's word be abrogated? No (Surah 6:115; 6:34; 10:64). Yes (Surah 2:106; 16:101).

- Was Pharaoh drowned or saved when chasing the Israelites? Saved (Surah 10:92). Drowned (Surah 28:40; 17:103; 43:55).

All of these instances (and many others) call into question the accuracy of the Qur'an.

The Accuracy of the Qur'an

Most Muslims believe that the Qur'an has been perfectly preserved and that there remains only one Qur'an.

> No other book in the world can match the Qur'an . . . The astounding fact about this book of Allah is that it has remained

unchanged, even to a dot, over the last fourteen hundred years ... No variation of text can be found.[6]

When asked about this, most Muslims will readily agree. When pressed further, many will say that the perfect text is only available in Arabic. And while it is true that Islam approves only of versions of the Qur'an in Arabic, the Qur'an has been passed down through many transmitted Arabic versions. You cannot recite or read the Qur'an except through one of these various versions. Each version has its own chain of transmission like the hadith. Officially, there are seven authoritative texts called "readers" (*qurra'*)[7] whose text is accepted by Islamic scholarship. The authoritative "readers" are:

Nafi;

Ibu Kathir;

Abu 'Amr al-'Ala';

Ibu 'Amir;

Hamzah;

al-Qisa'i; and,

Abu Bakr' Asim. [8]

These Arabic versions contain vast differences. In fact, in one section of the Qur'an, Surah 2, there are over 140 conflicting and variant readings of the Arabic text. A listing of the variant readings of this one surah requires over 90 pages of single spaced type to

---

6 *Basic Principles of Islam*, p. 4.

7 In addition to "The Seven Readers," listed above there are another group called "The Three" which include Abu Ja'far, Ya'qub al-Hashimi, and Khalaf al-Bazzar. Still other Islamic groups recognize four additional texts called "The Four," which include Muhaysin, al-Yazidi, al-Hasan al-Basri, and al-A'mash. More information on these readers can be found in *The Different Arabic Versions of the Qur'an* by Samuel Green, www.answering-islam.org.

8 In actuality, there are many more than 80 transmitted Arabic versions, but their chain of narration is considered weak.

record the differences.[9] In all, approximately two thirds of the verses in the Qur'an have some type of accepted variant. Said conversely, only one third of the verses in the Qur'an have no significant variant readings. In all, there are over 4,000 accepted variants among the accepted readers of the Qur'an.[10]

What makes matters interesting is that variant readings are recognized by Muslim "scholars" as of equal authority (even if opposing views are present). Many of the variant readings are considered binding depending on whether or not a Caliphate[11] has been established in a certain area or not.[12] In addition to the variants that the "readers" provide, within 200 years of Muhammed, over 600,000 "hadiths," (sayings of Muhammed) from outside the Qur'an were collected which interpreters debate over and insert into their individual versions of the Qur'an.

Although Muslims believe that the Qur'an is only to be read in Arabic, and while many Muslims will condemn all non-Arabic versions as unholy and sacrilege, more than 90 percent of Muslims around the world do not know Arabic, and even fewer know Qur'anic Arabic—therefore they cannot read the Qur'an[13] or they must use a

9 This is truly amazing when you consider that the Surah begins with the words, "This is the Scripture whereof there is no doubt . . ." (Surah 2:2). In that one verse alone, there are literally dozens of variants.

10 *The Encyclopedia of the Quranic Readings with an Introduction to Readings and Famous Readers*, is a six-volume encyclopedia set which records all known variants. For more information on this, see www.answering-islam.org.

11 See discussion of Medina and Mecca Muslims.

12 For example, the version (reader) used in Algeria, Morocco, West Africa and Sudan is different than the one used in Qatar, which is different than one used in Yemen, which is different than the one used in Afghanistan.

13 Few Muslims have actually read their own holy book. There are several reasons why Muslims do not read the Qur'an. First, illiteracy among Muslims is very high. In some Muslim nations seventy-five to eighty percent of the people cannot read or write. Second, many Muslims are too poor to own a copy of the Qur'an. Third, the Qur'an is not emphasized as a spiritual discipline. Knowledge of the Qur'an is not one of the five pillars of Islam that Muslims

translation. Many English translations exist. These also vary greatly. Some English translations of the Qur'an intentionally soften language in an attempt to make statements and beliefs more palatable to those in the West. A list of versions that are frequently referred to include the following translations by: Mirzal Abu'l Fadl, Muhammed Asad, T.B. Irving, Muhammed Marmaduke William Pickthall, Abdullah Yusuf Ali, S.M. Sarwar, M.H. Shakir, Al-Hajj Hafiz Ghulam Sarwar, Mohsin Khan, Abdul Majid Daryabadi, Zafarullah Khan, Kamuluddin and Nazir Ahmad, Salahuddin Peer, Malik Ghulam Farid, Khadim Rahman Nuri, Firozuddin Ruhl, N.J. Dawood, and A.J. Arberry—to name just a few.[14]

To make matters more difficult, many translations do not number either verses or paragraphs. Those which do divide the text into chapters (*surahs*) and verses (*'ayats*) do not follow a standard. Therefore the text is numbered differently in various versions and are inconsistent in both English and Arabic. Because of these facts, it is impossible to quote the Qur'an accurately and consistently. To be scholarly, you must consult all translations to find a dominant wording. Even if you can find a consistent text—Islam teaches that this still doesn't matter. Language is irrelevant. Ultimately, a person cannot understand the Qur'an unless it is revealed to them by Allah.[15]

> Qur'an was revealed in Arabic but God promised to be its teacher ... and the One to explain it. God told us that language is irrelevant, and that only the sincere ones are going to understand the Qur'an irrespective of their language, while those who are not

---

are expected to observe. Finally, Muslims believe the Qur'an must be read in Arabic and even modern Arabic speakers do not necessarily know Qur'anic Arabic.

14 These are not simply differences as a result of translation from a common text, but translations of various copies of the Qur'an.

15 For example, Surah 2:1 reads, "*Alif-Lam-Mim*. These letters are one of the miracles of the Quran and none but Allah Alone knows their meanings."

sincere or failed to worship Him ALONE will fail to understand it (even if they speak, read and write Arabic). Trust God and know that He is the teacher of the Qur'an.[16]

Overall, it is commonplace to hear that Muslims should learn to discover the meaning of the Qur'an in Arabic because it is undignified unless it is in the Arabic language. It is said that there cannot be an accurate and faithful expression of the Holy Qur'an in the English language (or any other language) because it is unable to match the majesty, grandeur, and perfection of the language of heaven.[17]

---

16 Dr. Rashad Khalifa, *Qur'an, Hadith and Islam*.

17 Although it is suggested that the Qur'an can only be truly understood in Arabic because it alone can capture its true meaning, the Qur'an is not written in perfect Arabic but has many grammatical errors and non-Arabic words. Many parts of the Qur'an have been lost and added throughout the years (entire verses and chapters). In response to this, it is not uncommon to hear that the perfect Qur'an resides only in heaven and is not available on earth.

Ten

Women in Islam

Muslim women are always to be under the protection of a male relative: father, husband, brother, uncle, or son. It is argued that the more strictly she is controlled, the more highly she is valued. Because of this, it is common that a woman needs to ask permission even to be allowed to visit her mother or sister, and she will rarely be allowed to visit alone.

In Islam, the woman's place is in the home. Her primary role is to produce sons for her husband, to care for them, and to do housework. In some rare instances, a woman will be allowed to work outside the home if the family finances make this a necessity.[1]

Clothing

Islam teaches that a woman must dress modestly. This normally means covering herself from the neck to the ankle as well as the wrist. Modesty also includes covering her hair. Different cultures fulfill these criteria in different ways, but the covering should always be opaque and loose-fitting. Long, unbound hair is considered immodest.

---

1 This is more accepted in Western cultures.

In some parts of the world the feet, hands, and face are also required to be covered in public. While brightly-colored clothing may be worn at home, a dark outer garment is almost always required when going outside.

The *hijab* (head-covering which often includes a veil) is often of great interest. In conservative Islamic countries such as Saudi Arabia, the hijab is mandatory. In more secular countries it is not required in certain contexts. In the West this is becoming a point of controversy.

Marriage

Marriage is seen in the Qur'an as a gift from Allah (Surah 16:72) and is what is expected of all females (Surah 4:25). Singleness is shunned and often considered an indication of immorality. Childbearing is also considered a gift of Allah and voluntary childlessness is unheard of in most Islamic circles.

Marriage is not simply the joining of a husband and a wife, but a joining of the respective families. Because of this, marriages are almost exclusively arranged by the families and there is often very little consultation with the couple who is to be married. On some occasions they will not even be allowed to see each other until the wedding day. In some circumstances, the bride is not required to be present at the contract ceremony but can be represented by a male relative. It is also very unusual to find a happy bride. A happy bride is considered improper (tears of sadness are required to show how much she will miss her family). While the bride is supposed to be unhappy during the wedding ceremony, an unhappy wife is considered a disgrace to her family after the wedding. In some instances, a family will even prevent a woman from returning home no matter how badly she is being treated by her husband or her in-laws.

While a Muslim man is permitted to marry a Christian or a Jewish woman (although she will from then on be considered a Muslim), a Muslim woman can only marry a Muslim man. A woman is taught to look to her sons for love and nurture, rather than to her husband who is to be seen as her provider and her protector.

Muhammed and Women

A careful study of Muhammed and his treatment of women is quite disturbing. Here are but a few examples. While the Qur'an allows Muslims to marry a maximum of four wives (Surah 4:3), Muhammed, who had received a special revelation from Allah, had at least eleven wives at one time and married a total of fifteen,[2] with at least four additional concubines. One of Muhammed's wives, named Aisha, was only nine years old when the fifty-two year old prophet consummated the marriage. Another of Muhammed's wives, Zainab, was originally married to his adopted son Zaid before Allah told him to take her as his own wife.

In addition to marriage and divorce, Muhammed allowed his followers to possess an unlimited number of sex slaves (Surah 23:5-6; 70:22-30) and allowed for prostitution through the institution of temporary marriage.[3]

Muhammed also declared that women were mentally deficient to men and that hell will primarily be inhabited by women because they are so ungrateful to their husbands.[4]

2 Several other women had a type of marriage contract with Muhammed but due to legal technicalities they never became full wives. At least ten other women received marriage proposals but for various reasons did not marry. Still others will be married to Muhammed in paradise.

3 Sahih Bukhari 6.60.139; Sahih Muslim 3248.

4 Sahih Bukhari 2.18.1616.

Other Concerns

The inequalities between men and women are clearly seen in the following overview of Islamic beliefs and practices.

- The Qur'an commands men to physically discipline wives (Surah 4:34).

- Men are by creation superior to women.

- Women are deficient in intelligence.

- Women are incapable of legal testimony.

- Women are described as animals or toys.

- Women are to be ('awrat) ashamed of their body. They should veil their body.

- Men are permitted multiple wives and sexual rights to slaves.

- Men can have four wives (Surah 4:3).

- Men are permitted divorce.

- Divorce can happen within four hours of marriage without question.

- With extenuating circumstances or "hardship," divorce can be done in one or two hours.

- All that is required for a man to divorce his wife is that he says three times, "I divorce you."

- Women cannot divorce a man.

- Muhammed had many wives by special permission from Allah.

Where are those who champion women's rights? Where are those who say that other religions, including Christianity, are sexist? Why do they remain silent?

Eleven

Violence and Islam

Everyone seems to think that Islam means "peace."[1] Even former president of the United States Barack Obama, and former prime minister of Great Britain David Cameron, have said so repeatedly. Secretary of State Hillary Clinton, many members of Congress, and of course the nightly news are more than willing to give voice to this inaccuracy. It is common to hear that "the terrorists who hijacked the planes also hijacked Islam." What is amazing is that the peacefulness of Islam is most frequently voiced directly following the continued acts of violence.

But where did this sentiment that Islam means peace come from? It might surprise you to know that the phrase "Islam is a religion of peace," did not even appear until the 20th century. It is certainly not used in the Qur'an nor in the Hadith, nor is it taught in Islamic cultures outside of the West. The phrase was first used in the title of a 1930 book in India and received immediate resistance from the Islam community itself. The phrase, however, was picked up by a few Islamic authors, and by the 1970s began to appear more fre-

---

1 See the full discussion of this in Chapter One and Islam's nomenclature.

quently in books that were designed for Western audiences.[2] Today, many American Muslims are taught by their Imams and family that Islam is a religion of peace—and many, maybe even most American Muslims do want to live a peaceful life, take care of their families, and worship Allah. This narrative of peace is one that most American Muslims try to convey.

It is common to read the following description: Muhammed lived a very meek and humble life and preached a peaceful message— inviting people to accept Islam and only fighting defensive battles when necessary. Islam is not only portrayed as a religion of peace, but Muhammed is championed as a merciful conqueror and a man whose life and character prove that he is a prophet. But this is not what history records, nor is it the record of even the most respected hadith in the Muslim world. Investigate from primary sources of Islam and you will find that Islam is anything but a religion of peace.

Muhammed and Violence

Contrary to what we Westerners are often asked to believe, Muhammed's life was fraught with warfare and battle.[3] Muhammed said that fighting is literally the greatest thing in the world.[4] In fact, he boldly pronounced that nothing in Islam earns a Muslim more reward than fighting in battle. Muhammed considered fighting in jihad more righteous than praying without ceasing or fasting perpetually.[5] Muhammed even taught that dying in battle is so great an

---

2 See Nabeel Qureshi and his book *Answering Jihad* for details about the development of the phrase "Islam is a religion of peace."

3 This in itself should not disqualify Muhammed because some in the Bible, like Joshua, also practiced warfare. But Muhammed took conquest to a new level.

4 Sahih Bukhari 4.52.50. Sahih Bukhari is considered to be one of the most trusted sources of hadith in Islam.

5 Sahih Bukhari 4.52.44.

activity that it would make a man desire to leave heaven to continue fighting.[6]

As far as Muhammed's involvement, he personally led his people into battle each of the last ten years of his life, fighting in over 80 wars. During those battles he would invoke curses upon his enemies, encourage his people to denigrate nonbelievers, send assassins to kill his enemies in their sleep, and personally assassinate those who disagreed with him.[7] He often participated by cutting off the hands and feet of his enemies and branding their eyes with a heated iron.[8] He led battles against unarmed cities, commanded children to be killed during nighttime raids, and collected women as slaves to be used in sexual conquest.

Far from fighting only defensive battles, Muhammed proclaimed, "I have been ordered to fight ... until they testify that none has the right to be worshiped but Allah,"[9] and, "I will expel the Jews and Christians from the Arabian Peninsula and will not leave any but Muslim."[10]

No one can legitimately argue, based on the hadith, that Muhammed was a man of peace. But the violence of Muhammed is not simply relegated to the hadith.

The Qur'an and Violence

According to the Qur'an, Muhammed was a man of war. He led armies. He ordered his enemies killed. He never shrank from bloodshed.

6 Sahih Bukhari 4.52.72.

7 Sahih Bukhari 5:59.297; 5:59.449.

8 Sahih Bukhari 7.71.589.

9 Sahih Bukhari 1.2.25.

10 Sahih Muslim 1767. Sahih Muslim is also considered one of the most trustworthy sources among the hadith by Muslims.

He that leaves his dwelling to fight for God and His apostle and is then overtaken by death, shall be rewarded by God (Surah 4:100).

Deal rigorously with unbelievers (Surah 9:73).

Open the pages of the Qur'an and you can literally find hundreds of examples:[11]

Slay the pagans where ever you find them (Surah 2:191).

I will instill terror into the hearts of the unbelievers, smite ye above their necks and smite all their fingertips off them. It is not ye who slew them; it was God (Surah 8:13-17).

Fight and slay the pagans wherever ye find them and seize them, beleaguer them, and lie in wait for them, in every stratagem . . . (Surah 9:5).

Fight those who do not believe in God and the last day . . . and fight People of the Book (Christians and Jews) who do not accept the religion of truth (Islam) until they pay tribute by hand, being inferior (Surah 9:29).

O true believers, when you encounter the unbelievers, strike off their heads (Surah 47:4).

Unbelievers are entitled to no compassion (Surah 48:29).

One of the oaths of some Muslims goes like this:

I state in the presence of God that I will slaughter infidels my entire life . . . May God give me strength in fulfilling this oath.[12]

There are no mitigating verses prescribing mercy toward unbe-

---

11 For more details about Jihad in the Qur'an, see Appendix C.

12 *Islam Unveiled*, 1.

lievers.[13] On the contrary, the Qur'an is full of elaborate instructions on the conduct of war, the methods of executing the infidels, and the rewards that will accrue to those martyred in a holy war.

The words "fight" and "kill" appear in the Qur'an more frequently than the word "pray." To isolate Islamic terrorists as "Muslim fundamentalists" is absurd. Muslim fundamentalists and terrorists are merely pushing their doctrine to its logical end. There is no Muslim version of: "Love your enemies, and pray for those who persecute you" (Matthew 5:44) or "If anyone strikes you on the right cheek, turn to him the other also" (Matthew 5:39).[14] Therefore, speaking freely against Islam is very risky.

> Whoever by words, either spoken or written, or by visible representation, or by imputation, innuendo, or insinuation, directly or indirectly defiles the sacred name of the Holy Prophet Muhammed . . . shall be punished with death . . .[15]

Again, there are certainly many American Muslims who have been taught by their Imams and family that Islam is a religion of peace. But if they would take the time to investigate this from the primary sources, they would quickly discover that Islam is indeed a forceful religion. Upon this discovery, a Muslim has only one of three options: apathy, apostasy, or radicalization.

Furthermore, those who remain ambivalent about the nature of Islam and continue to take a peaceful or moderate view of Islam

---

13 Some Muslims will put forward verses of peace and compromise. It is important to read these verses in context and also remember the principle of abrogation. At a minimum, abrogation says that the later pronouncements nullify the earlier ones (Surah 9 is among the last, if not the last of the surahs). Most Islamic scholars classify surahs according to whether they were uttered in Mecca or Medina and give a different set of instructions depending on the strength of Islam in the area.

14 For more information on The Bible and Violence see Appendix D.

15 Quoted in *Islam Unveiled*, p. 32.

need to realize that they are themselves at risk! They need to read the many passages which speak about the Muslim who will not take the Qur'an literally or who tries to soften its words. The moderate Muslim is to be dealt with more harshly than even the unbeliever.

It should also be restated that some who appear to have taken a more "moderate" view have simply taken a "long view." Their ultimate goal is to establish a Caliphate and institute Sharia law, at which point everything changes.

Islam and Persecution

In many countries where Islam is dominant, all religious observance outside of Islam is prohibited. Members of other religions are not even allowed to meet together. In other Islamic countries, it is considered a crime to convert to Judaism or Christianity.

Although some Muslims assert that Islam is tolerant of other religions, persecution always exists against non-Muslims when Islam becomes prevalent.

In 2000, *Open Doors* magazine published its "Top Ten List" of the "worst persecutors of Christians." Seven of the ten "Worst Offenders" were Muslim nations. In 2002, fifteen of the top twenty "Worst Offender" nations were Muslim nations.

And it is not isolated to foreign countries. There are literally dozens of web sites in the United States devoted to Islamic persecution of Christians—here in our country.[16]

---

16 Being from Idaho, I was shocked to learn of one such site on the campus of the University of Idaho.

Conclusion: Part One

We hear often that Muslim terrorists are "radical Muslims" or even "Muslim extremists." Both labels are used to convey the idea that there is a small fringe group of Muslims who have hijacked and distorted Islam. In the same vein, we are told that true Islam is a peaceful religion. Three of our most recent presidents—Presidents Clinton, Bush, and Obama—have called Islam a "religion of peace" in an attempt to distinguish between Islamic terrorists and "moderate" Muslims. But are these accurate and appropriate conclusions?

The most powerful and influential leaders in the Islamic world do not make this distinction between radical Muslims and moderate Muslims. For example, Turkish Prime Minister Recep Tayyip Erdogan called the term moderate Islam "a very ugly term." He said, "It is offensive and an insult to our religion. There is no moderate or immoderate Islam. Islam is Islam and that's it."[1]

While it may be politically correct to make such distinctions, the argument over radical and moderate Muslims is flawed at its very core. Let me highlight just a few problems by asking a few questions.

---

1 Daniel Pipes, "Erdogan: Turkey Is Not a Country Where Moderate Islam Prevails," June 14, 2004. Www.danielpipes.org/blog/2004/06/erdo287an-turkey-is-not-a-country-where.

1. What distinguishes radical Muslims from those who are moderate? Do radical Muslims believe in the Qur'an and see Muhammed as their prophet while moderate Muslims do not? No, from all indications, both radical and moderate Muslims believe in the Qur'an and see Muhammed as their prophet.

2. If radical and moderate Muslims both believe the Qur'an and the Hadith, then is it only the radical Muslims who fully believe and totally commit themselves to the teaching of the Qur'an and the Hadith, while the moderate Muslims do not fully believe or commit to the teachings of the Qur'an and the Hadith? If this is the case, then aren't the true-believing Muslims actually the radical Muslims and the moderate Muslims only nominal Muslims? Should we classify nominal Muslims as true Muslims any more than we classify nominal Christians as true Christians? Would we praise nominal Christians for not being fully committed to the principles of their faith?

3. If radical Muslims are those who engage in terror and the killing of innocent people, then in order to be consistent, should we not classify Muhammed (and the first four caliphs) as a radical Muslim because he was Islam's first warrior? Should not those who follow the example of Muhammed be considered the followers of true Islam?

4. How do radical Muslims become radical? Is it not through the literal reading of the Qur'an and the Hadith? Doesn't all of Islam require a literal reading of the Qur'an and the Hadith? Anyone who has read the Qur'an understands that the Qur'an never advocates or tolerates Islam to be practiced in moderation.

5. Is the desire to be governed by Sharia law and to establish a caliphate only a belief of radical Muslims or is the adoption of Sharia law an ambition of all Muslims, whether radical or moderate?

6. When Islam takes a place of prominence in a country (or even a specific region), is a moderate view of Islam tolerated by other followers of Islam or is it rejected?

When faced with these questions, one must conclude that either radical Muslims are the true Muslims while moderate Muslims are nominal Muslims, or that there is a deeper understanding of Islam that needs to be recognized. This deeper understanding recognizes the difference between Mecca Muslims and Medina Muslims. *Islam allows and even encourages Muslims to practice a more tolerant approach to non-Muslims until Islam reaches a point of prominence.* When this happens, the true character of Islam is always revealed.

Part Two

A Christian's Response: How to Witness to Our Muslim Neighbors

Twelve

Setting the Tone

In Part One, I attempted to give you the truth about the faith, practices, and beliefs of Islam. But as Christians, it's not enough to know the truth about Muslims—we need to put our knowledge into action. We need to put the truth into practice. We need to understand Islam AND be willing to share the Good News of the Gospel.

Jesus came to turn people from darkness to light. And if darkness refers to people outside of Christ—if you are going by sheer numbers—the Muslim world wins the "darkness award" hands down. With more than 1.57 billion followers who have put their faith in Allah—there is no greater mission field in the world than the Muslim community.

Did you know that approximately 80 percent of Muslims worldwide have never heard the Good News, making Muslims the least evangelized people in the world? And as Christians, we need to be ready. That being said, what can you do? Let me start by giving you three brief suggestions.

Gain Their Respect

As mentioned earlier, most Muslims associate the American lifestyle with Christian values, thinking that they are one and the same. Christians suffer from guilt by association. Part of their perceptions are that Westerners, especially Americans (and therefore Christians by association), are superficial in their friendships and not particularly willing to open their hearts, homes, and kitchens. In order for you to reach them, you must first build a relationship with them. Conversation, trust, and respect are vital to this process.

The simplest way to begin this process is by loving your neighbor. If you know Muslims—love them. While we may not love what is done in the name of Islam, we are to love Muslims in the name of Christ. As they see the love of Christ lived through your life, they will be compelled by the person of Christ in you.

But beyond your love of Christ, you need to demonstrate your commitment to Christ!

There is a reason why Islam is growing so rapidly. They are committed to their faith. There is much we could learn from them, and need to learn from them, if we are going to reach them. To earn their respect you must consider the following:

- Their dedication to prayer—five times a day.
- Their life of submission to Allah's commands.
- Their honor and reverence to Allah.
- Their commitment to fasting and dietary laws.
- Their willingness to help those in need.
- Their zeal for the cause of Allah.

In light of these considerations, it may prove helpful for you to:
- Engage in regular prayer five times a day. If given the oppor-

tunity, explain why it is not necessary for you to face Mecca, but can pray in any direction.

- Give generously to the physical needs of others. Be the first on the scene to help someone who is struggling or in need.[1]

- Be hospitable, opening your home to them. Show genuine love for them and be sensitive to their dietary restrictions (i.e., Muslims do not eat pork or drink alcohol).[2]

- Place an emphasis on your family (both immediate and extended family).

- Avoid confrontation.

- Find out what they believe. You should not tell them what they believe; they may actually not believe (or know) what Islam teaches.

- Know Islam better than they know it.

- Show reverence for the Bible. A Muslim would never think of underlining or making notations in the Qur'an, nor would they ever set it on the floor. When working with them, use an unmarked, well-cared-for copy of the Bible.

- Be careful of opposite-sex friendships. Here are some additional comments on this subject. Any conversation with the opposite sex, should be at the Muslim's initiative. In addition, never touch anyone of the opposite sex (even to shake hands), unless the other person initiates it. Try to

---

1 Whatever your belief about refugees entering the United States, we should reach out and care for those who are already here.

2 In addition, Muslims can only eat meat from an animal that has been slaughtered by a Muslim in the proper way. This requires the one performing the act to face Mecca and say the name of Allah aloud. The animal cannot be hungry or thirsty at the time of the slaughter, and the knife cannot be sharpened in front of the animal. In addition, animals that have been killed by strangulation, falling, beating, or found dead cannot be eaten.

avoid eye contact with the opposite sex, even if a conversation develops.

- Dress modestly. This is especially true for women. Close fitting or tight clothing will immediately create a barrier.

- Put your dog away—while you may consider them to be part of your family, most Muslims consider them unclean.[3]

- Practice Christian behavior in everything you do.

Find Common Ground

There are similarities on which you can talk with Muslims. I am not suggesting that you gloss over differences or minimize Christian essentials, but I am suggesting there are many points of agreement where you can begin a fruitful dialogue. Let me give a word of caution here. Do not let major differences go undiscussed—simply pointing out the similarities will cause more harm than good. It would be more beneficial in the long run to have pointed out the distinctions between the two faiths, than to leave a conversation with the impression that both faiths believe essentially the same thing—they do not.

Still, to get a conversation going, it may be helpful to start with commonalities with the understanding that many of the initial points of contact are the very issues where we need to examine critical differences.

At a surface level, Islam and Christianity do have points of contact. Here are a few of the commonalities:

- Both faiths are monotheistic.[4]

_____

3 It is permissible to keep pets (birds, fish, reptiles), but Muslims cannot keep pigs or dogs, or any animal which may cause harm to another. The domestic cat is a revered animal in Islam and was praised by the prophet Muhammed.

4 Monotheism is the belief in one God. Muslims do not understand that Christians believe in one God in three persons. You must clarify this for them. This will be discussed in Chapter Thirteen.

- Both believe in an eternal, all-powerful, all-knowing God who is sovereign over the universe.

- Both believe that God created mankind out of one man and one woman.

- Both believe in a resurrection and a day of final judgment.

But the similarities between the two faiths run even deeper.

- Both trace their lineage through Abraham.

- Both believe in the prophets of the Old and New Testaments.

- Both believe that God has given Scripture to lead and guide us.

- Both teach that Satan is a deceiver who wants to mislead.

- Both teach that believers should care for each other.

- Both teach the importance of proclaiming the truth to nonbelievers.

Perhaps the most surprising commonality is the reverence both display for Jesus.

- Both teach that Jesus was born of a virgin.

- Both believe that he was a worker of miracles.

- Both believe that Jesus cleansed lepers, healed the blind, and even raised the dead.

- Both teach that Jesus is the Messiah.

- Both believe that Jesus was sinless.

- Both are awaiting Jesus' return.

These areas of common ground might be a good starting point for your dialogues. But remember, just because there are similarities does not mean that our differences are insignificant.[5] But by beginning with points of commonality, you can begin inserting key elements into your conversation. For example, as you talk about God and his sovereignty (they will respect this language)—emphasize God's love and mercy—this may be unfamiliar but attractive to them. When you talk about sin and the need for salvation—point out that salvation is knowable. If the topic of Jesus comes up—use the analogy of Jesus as the Lamb of God sacrificed for our sins.[6]

Lift Up Jesus

Most Muslims who come to Christ are not won over by intellectual arguments which disprove the validity of Islam. Rather, they are won by the message of Jesus Christ as presented by a Christian friend. As they learn about Jesus, they will begin to discover a critical difference between Islam and Christianity. Muslims must understand that Christianity is not just a religion, but a personal relationship with Jesus Christ.

The following chapters will help you have meaningful dialogue with your Muslim neighbors.

---

5 We will go into greater detail about these issues later.

6 During the pilgrimage, a lamb is offered to Allah.

Thirteen

Sharing Your Faith

I n the close of the last chapter it was stated that most Muslims who come to Christ are not primarily won over by intellectual arguments, however, a working knowledge of Islam and an accurate understanding of Christianity are essential in having a meaningful dialogue.

Most Muslims do not have an accurate view of Christianity. Some of the biggest stumbling blocks for Muslims include their mistaken belief that Christians worship three gods, that the term "Son of God" as applied to Jesus is a physical description, and that Christians have corrupted their Scriptures. These and other issues will be addressed in the following chapters.

It is also important to remember that Muhammed is considered to be the last and greatest of the prophets. Simply attacking their prophet unnecessarily (or the message given to him in the Qur'an) may result in ending any useful dialogue prematurely. A better approach may be to steer the conversation toward Christ rather than criticize their prophet or their scripture.

In each case, as you begin conversations with your Muslim friends, it will be essential for you to correctly define terms and have a clear understanding of what your respective faiths actually believe. This clarification will not only aid in conversation, but will ultimately provide hope for those who are trapped in hopelessness.

So where should you begin? The simple answer is that you should begin where the conversation leads you. The three listed above (God, Jesus, and Scripture) are all good candidates. This chapter will focus on the topic of God.

Sharing Your Faith About God

It is essential to bring clarity to the basic concept of "God"—whom Muslims refer to as "Allah." Let me remind you that the word "Allah" is simply the Arabic word for God whether you are an Arab Muslim, an Arab Jew, or an Arab Christian—all use the same word. That is not to say, however, that Christians and Muslims worship the same God— they do not. Arab Christians and Muslims simply use the same word for God. It will be helpful in your conversations to clarify whose God you are talking about—the God of Islam, or the God of Christianity. At this point, I would encourage you to state the obvious: Christians worship Yahweh (in the form of the Trinity), while Islam worships Allah (whom they believe to be absolutely one without division of any kind).

God and the Trinity

One of the biggest contentions between Islam and Christianity is in regards to the Trinity.[1] Obviously, this is not an insignificant difference. Muslims believe that Allah is absolutely one and have the misunderstanding that Christians worship three Gods.[2]

---

1 Many Muslims have been taught to point out that the word "Trinity" is not even found in the Bible. This is certainly true. The concept of the Tri-unity of God, however, finds its way throughout its pages. It might be helpful to ask them if they believe in the concept of *tauheed* (the absolute oneness of Allah). They will readily admit this. Then you can point out that the word tauheed is not found in the Qur'an.

2 See Chapter Seven.

As we have seen, Islam makes every effort to condemn the Trinity as blasphemous (Surah 4:171). The Qur'an denies that Allah is a father (Surah 5:18) and that he has a son (Surah 112:3). The denial of the Trinity is a central doctrine of Islamic theology and to suggest that Allah has an equal is shirk—the greatest possible sin. As Christians, you first need to offer a simple and clear explanation that you also believe that God is one. Deuteronomy 6:4 reads, "Hear, O Israel: The LORD our God, the LORD is one." The Christian Trinity is not the belief in three Gods (tritheism), it is the belief in one God who manifests himself in three distinct, yet inseparable persons (i.e., the Father, the Son, and the Holy Spirit).[3]

In typical fashion, most Muslims will either respond that the belief in three in one is either contradictory, or that is too complex to be true. In regards to the latter, I would argue that by definition we cannot comprehend God. If God created our minds, he must be greater than our comprehension. A close examination of the former shows that a Christian belief in unity of "three persons" in "one God" is not a contradiction. A contradiction occurs when something is both "A" and "not A" at the same time and in the same sense. God is both three and one at the same time, but not in the same sense. God is three persons, but one in essence. God is three persons, but only one in nature or being.

It would be a contradiction to say that God had three natures in one nature, or that God was three persons in one person, or that God was three beings in one being. But it is not a contradiction to claim that God has three persons in one nature.[4]

---

3 Islam also inaccurately teaches that the Christian Trinity is composed of God, Mary, and Jesus.

4 For a fuller discussion of the topic of the Trinity, see my book *Email Messages: A Minister Answers Questions from His Congregation.*

This is no doubt a difficult topic, but a correction of the misunderstanding of Islam about the Trinity is not only essential, it can serve as the very foundation on which you can build your dialogue about the one, true God.

God as a Relational, Knowable Being

When Muslims say, *Allahu-Akbar*, they are stating that Allah is great. As Christians, we certainly agree with that. Both Muslims and Christians believe that God is the creator of the universe and therefore the greatest being. But in Islam, Allah's greatness requires that he be far removed from his creation and is in his very essence a non-relational being. Allah is so transcendent that it is impossible for man to know him intimately or to have a personal relationship with him. In Christianity, we believe that God created us because he is a relational being (as evidenced by the Trinity) and wants to be known by us.[5] This is again, great news! We can know him and be known by him. Our relationship with God, though severed by sin, has been reestablished through Jesus Christ. Because of Jesus we can truly know God. Once discovered, this will be a joyous occasion for your Muslim friends.

> And this is eternal life, that they know you the only true God, and Jesus Christ whom you have sent (John 17:3).

> I am the good shepherd; I know my own and my own know me (John 10:14).

> I keep asking ... that the God of our Lord Jesus Christ, the Father of glory, may give you the Spirit of wisdom and of revelation in the knowledge of him ... so that you may know what is the hope to which he has called you (Ephesians 1:17).

---

5 This might be a great topic of conversation. If Allah is not a relational being and he cannot be known, why did he create man in the first place? As Christians, God is a relational being who created us to have fellowship with him.

Beloved, let us love one another, for love is from God. And whoever loves has been born of God and knows God. Anyone who does not love does not know God, because God is love (1 John 4:7-8).

God as Father

In Islam, the thought of Allah as a personal father is repugnant and seen as blasphemous. This is especially true of a father-son relationship between God and Jesus which the Qur'an specifically denies.

> In the name of Allah, Most Gracious, Most Merciful. Say: He is Allah the One; Allah, the Eternal, Absolute: He begetteth not, nor is He begotten; And there is none like unto him (Surah 112:1-4).

The Qur'an erroneously assumes that the God of Christianity acquired a son through procreation—that is that God and Mary had sexual relations in order to conceive Jesus. You need to point out that Jesus is not God's son in a physical sense, but in a metaphysical sense. Make sure you point out that the Christian God is by his very nature a relational God and wants to have a relationship with us.

Christians as Children of God

> (Both) the Jews and the Christians say: "We are sons of Allah, and His beloved." Say: "Why then doth He punish you for your sins? Nay, ye are but men . . ." (Surah 5:18).

As Christians, we believe that we are children of God.

> But to all who did receive him, who believed in his name, he gave the right to become children of God, who were born, not of blood nor of the will of the flesh nor of the will of man, but of God (John 1:12-13).

> See what kind of love the Father has given to us, that we should be called children of God; and so we are (1 John 3:1).[6]

---

6 See also Romans 8:16, 21; 9:8; Philippians 2:15; 1 John 2:28; 3:10; 5:2; etc.

God as Love

Furthermore, Christians believe that we are loved by God. This may be one of the most effective means by which to bring a Muslim to Christ. In Islam, Allah is far removed and distant. Of all the 99 names of Allah, love is not among them. But as Christians, we believe that God, by his very nature, is love and he has demonstrated this love for us.

> For God so loved the world, that he gave his only Son, that whoever believes in him should not perish but have eternal life (John 3:16).

> But God shows his love for us in that while we were still sinners, Christ died for us (Romans 5:8).

> Anyone who does not love does not know God, because God is love (1 John 4:8).

The Qur'an stresses that Allah does not love the sinner. This is much different than the God of the Bible. While God does not love sin, he does indeed love the sinner—in fact he loves all sinners. Thus, the love of Allah and the love of the God of the Bible are distinct from each other.

> You see, at just the right time, when we were still powerless, Christ died for the ungodly . . . But God demonstrates his own love for us in this: While we were still sinners, Christ died for us (Romans 5:6, 8, 10).

Fourteen

Sharing Your Faith About Jesus

Muslims refer to the Qur'an as "The Eternal Word of God." They believe that Allah sent his eternal and preexistent word to man to reveal how man ought to live. While Christians do not hold the Qur'an in the same esteem, we do share the belief that God sent "The Eternal Word of God"[1] to us in the form of Jesus. This becomes a great point of dialogue between Christians and Muslims.[2]

Jesus (Isa) and the Qur'an

Muslims have a deep respect for Jesus, considering him to be a prophet of God. With this understanding, ask your Muslim friend to try a simple exercise. Have them find all the passages in the Qur'an that mention the name Muhammed and write down what they learn about him (Muhammed is only referred to by name four times in the

---

1 John 1:1-14.

2 If the Qur'an is preexistent, perfect and eternal, how is it different than Allah himself? Does this belief give Allah an equal? How is the belief in the Qur'an as the "Eternal Word of God" different than the Christian belief in Jesus as the "Eternal Word of God"?

Qur'an).[3] Then ask Muslims to find all the passages that talk about Jesus (Isa) and write down what they learn about him (Most do not realize that Jesus is mentioned by name or referred to 93 times in the Qur'an).[4] While it is not necessary for us to deal with all of these, let me give you a few examples from the Qur'an.

- According to the Qur'an, Jesus was miraculously born of a virgin,[5] Muhammed was not. Ask your Muslim friends why Jesus was miraculously born of a virgin. Many Muslims will admit that they do not know how to answer this question. Use Isaiah 7:14[6] to help answer that question for them.

- According to the Qur'an, the baby Jesus can speak from the cradle[7] (obviously this is not in the Bible, but it is in the Qur'an). Ask the question, "Was Muhammed able to speak from the cradle?"

- The Qur'an teaches that the child Jesus took some mud, fashioned the mud into the form of a bird, blew on the bird, and it began to fly.[8] According to the Qur'an, Jesus is able to create something out of nothing. Could Muhammed do this?

- According to the Qur'an, Jesus could heal the blind, cleanse

---

3 Surah 3:144; 33:40; 47:2; 48:29.

4 Surah 2:87, 136, 253; 3:45, 46, 48, 49, 50, 52, 55, 59, 84; 4:157, 163, 171, 172; 5:17, 46, 72, 75, 78, 110, 112, 114, 116; 6:85; 9:30, 31; 19:19, 20, 21, 22, 27, 30, 31, 32, 33, 34, 88, 91, 92; 21:91; 23:50; 33:7; 42:13, 57, 61, 63; 57:27; 61:6, 14. Some verses have more than one reference to Jesus.

5 Surah 19:19-21; 21:91.

6 "Therefore the LORD himself will give you a sign. Behold a virgin shall conceive and bear a son, and shall call his name Immanuel."

7 Surah 3:46.

8 Surah 3:49.

lepers, and bring the dead to life.[9] Did Muhammed demonstrate his ability to do these things?

- According to the Qur'an, Jesus was sinless.[10] Was Muhammed sinless? Actually, according to the Qur'an, Muhammed must ask for forgiveness for his past and future sins.[11] All the other prophets in the Qur'an committed sins. Only Jesus was righteous.

- The Qur'an also says that Jesus was taken to heaven bodily and is alive. He will return at the second coming.[12] Is Muhammed alive and will he return at the second coming? Why did Jesus remain alive while Muhammed did not?

The list above contains things that Jesus can do, but Muhammed cannot do. The Qur'an also testifies to the following about Jesus.

- Jesus was strengthened with Holy Spirit (Surah 2:87).

- Jesus was given revelation from God (Surah 19:30).

- Jesus was a miracle worker (Surah 2:253).

- Jesus was sent with the Gospel (Surah 5:46; 57:27).

- Muslims are told to obey Jesus (Surah 43:63).

In actuality, Islam reveres Jesus. In the Qur'an, Jesus is called Muhammed's "Lord" (Surah 89:22) and the Truth (Surah 2:91). The Qur'an describes Jesus as the "Word" of God (Surah 3:45; 4:171) and a "spirit proceeding from Allah" (Surah 4:171).

Ultimately, it is not the life of Jesus that Muslims object to, it is the death of Jesus.

---

9 Surah 3:49.

10 Surah 19:19.

11 Surah 48:2.

12 Surah 3:55.

The Cross of Christ

One of the hardest (and most important) aspects of Christianity for Muslims to grasp is the cross of Christ. The purpose of the cross is not comprehended by Muslims for a couple of reasons. First, they do not understand or even see a need for sacrifice for sins. You need to help your Muslim friends understand the Christian concept of death as a consequence for sin, and the significance of a sinless Jesus, lovingly paying the debt we owe.[13]

A second difficulty stems from a common Islamic belief that God would not allow one of his prophets to die such a shameful death. This second objection is easily discussed by simply asking a couple of questions. First, "Did God spare other Islamic prophets from death, much less agonizing death?"[14] Second, dying for your faith as a martyr is considered one of the greatest acts possible. "Why is the fact that Jesus died so objectionable, if dying for your faith is to be praised?"[15]

For Christians, Christ crucified is at the very heart of the gospel (1 Corinthians 2:2). The Apostle Paul rested his whole case on the bodily resurrection of Christ from the dead. If Jesus rose from the dead, it was the most important event in all of history.

On the other hand, if Christ did not rise from the dead, the cross of Christ is nothing more than an interesting museum piece, a curiosity and nothing more. If Christ did not rise, Christianity has no objective validity or reality. If Christ did not rise, those martyrs

---

13 Romans 3:23; 6:23.

14 While some prophets, like Daniel, were rescued from death, many were viciously killed and slaughtered. Amos was killed with a staff. Jeremiah and Habakkuk were killed by stoning. Ahijah was killed by a lion. Zechariah son of Berachiah was killed by the sword and his blood sprinkled upon an altar. John the Baptist had his head cut off. Even Muhammed died because a Jewish woman fed him a poisoned piece of lamb at Khaibar. See Saheeh Bukhari, Volume 3, Book 47, Hadith 786, or Volume 4, Book 53, Hadith 394. (See also Hebrews 11:37.)

15 It is not the resurrection that troubles Muslims. Most Muslims believe in miracles. If Allah wanted to raise a person from the dead, he could surely do it.

who went singing to the lions' den, those Christians who were used to light the coliseum in Rome, our contemporary missionaries who have given their lives to spreading the gospel message, are nothing more than deluded fools.

This is why those who often attack Christianity concentrate their attack on the death, burial, and resurrection of Jesus. It is the crux of Christianity. But here is where Islam departs from the many others who deny the resurrection of Jesus. Muslims deny the resurrection *because* they deny that Jesus actually died on the cross. The Qur'an says:

> That they said (in boast), "We killed Christ Jesus the son of Mary, the Messenger of Allah";- but they killed him not, nor crucified him, but so it was made to appear to them, and those who differ therein are full of doubts, with no (certain) knowledge, but only conjecture to follow, for of a surety they killed him not (Surah 4:157).

The common saying among Muslims is: "Jesus did not die on the cross, it only appeared that he did." Two basic explanations are given as to what happened. The first says that Jesus did not die, he only appeared to die. The second says that it was not Jesus who died, but someone else died in his place. Let's take a look briefly at both of these views.

Jesus Did Not Die on the Cross: He Only Appeared Dead

Some Muslims believe that Jesus went to the cross, but did not die—it only appeared that Jesus died on the cross. This theory is referred to by some as the "Swoon Theory" which suggests that Jesus was mistakenly pronounced dead, but in the coolness of the tomb, he revived. When Jesus came out of the tomb and appeared to his disciples, they mistakenly thought he had risen from the dead.

But is it really possible to believe this theory? Is it likely that the Roman soldiers did not ensure that Jesus was truly dead? How do you explain the water and blood from Jesus' side when the soldiers thrust their spear? Is it possible to believe that a nearly-dead Jesus could have survived three days in a dark, cold tomb without food or water or attention of any kind to his medical ailments? Would Jesus have survived being wrapped in spice-laden graveclothes which were intended to mummify? Would Jesus have the strength to extricate himself from the burial shroud, push the heavy stone away from the mouth of the grave, overcome the Roman guards who stood watch at the tomb, and walk several miles on feet that had been pierced with spikes? Is it possible that this weakened Jesus could convince the disciples that he had miraculously been raised from the dead and that they could have new life in him? Most importantly, are we to believe that Jesus himself (who is considered sinless by both Christians and Muslims) was involved in a flagrant lie which encouraged his disciples to preach a false message that he had risen from the dead?

This theory is not in keeping with the facts of history, nor the commonly held beliefs of either Christians or Muslims.

Jesus Did Not Die on the Cross: Someone Else Did

The most widely-held Muslim view is that Allah substituted someone in the place of Jesus. Most Muslims believe that when the Roman soldiers came to Jesus by night in the Garden of Gethsemane,[16] Allah took Jesus up to heaven before the soldiers came to arrest him. Jesus was not arrested, he was never crucified, and therefore, he did not

---

16 A small portion of Muslims believe that Jesus was crucified but did not die on the cross—he simply appeared to die.

need to rise again. The man who died on the cross, was not Jesus, but a substitute for Jesus.[17]

Islamic scholars differ on who died on the cross. Some argue that Judas Iscariot was crucified in Jesus' place. Others suggest that it was Simon of Cyrene. Another theory is that one of the disciples volunteered to be crucified in Jesus' place. In each case, it is suggested that the likeness of Jesus was supernaturally transferred to the man who took Jesus' place. Most often, God substituted the face of Jesus on the other man's head.

But this theory fails to explain the resurrection appearances of Christ. Jesus appeared repeatedly to witnesses following the death, burial, and resurrection accounts. These appearances occurred from the morning of his resurrection to his ascension forty days later. Ten distinct appearances are recorded for us. These records show great variety as to time, place, and people. Jesus appeared to Peter and James. He appeared to the disciples as a group. At one point he spoke to a crowd of 500 who were assembled together. He appeared to Mary, Martha, and others.

The appearances were at different places. Some were in the garden near his tomb. Some were in the Upper Room. One was on the road from Jerusalem to Emmaus. One was as far away as Galilee. Each appearance was characterized by different acts and words by Jesus. The first two witnesses were women. This is important, because according to Jewish principles of legal evidence (as with Islamic law), women were not considered to be the best witnesses. They did not have a right to give testimony. If the story was manufactured, the women would never have been included in the story (at least not as the first witnesses).

17 It is more than a little ironic that Christianity teaches that God substituted Jesus for mankind, while Islam teaches that God substituted man for Jesus.

The resurrection appearances included miracles, meals, and ministry mandates. Was Judas now doing miracles and giving the marching orders to the disciples? Did the face of the Jewish Jesus transfixed on the body of Simon from Cyrene,[18] or anyone else, really fool anyone?

By all accounts of ancient history, the reports of Jesus' death on the cross are unshakable. It is the testimony of the soldiers, the witnesses at the foot of the cross, and the disciples that Jesus died on the cross and rose again.

Why Does It Matter?

In speaking with your Muslim friend, you will need to center your testimony on the cross of Christ. You must point out the consequence of sin, and the fact that God loved us so much that he sent Jesus to pay the price for our sin. You must point out that "All have sinned and fall short of the glory of God"[19] and that "the wages of sin is death."[20] Most of all, point out that God demonstrated his love for us in this, while we were sinners Christ died for us.[21]

Your Muslim neighbor needs to hear with clarity the simple news of the Gospel of Jesus Christ.

---

18 Cyrene was an ancient city in Libya. Simon, quite possibly, had dark skin.

19 Romans 3:23.

20 Romans 6:23.

21 Romans 5:8.

Fifteen

Sharing Your Faith—The Inerrancy of the Bible

I slam teaches that parts of the Bible were a revelation from Allah, but it has become distorted or corrupted (*tahrif*). They believe that much of the current text of the Bible was added later and not part of the original revelation/writing. Muslims conclude that the Bible, as it now stands, is invalid and untrustworthy because it is so corrupted, since the original Scriptures were lost. But are their conclusions legitimate?

The Accuracy of the Bible

While Muslims claim that the Bible has been tampered with, historical facts prove that the Bible has been neither tampered with nor corrupted. Modern critical scholars declare:

> The Bible says exactly what the autographs[1] contained—line

---

1 An autograph copy refers to the original manuscript that was penned by the author himself, rather than a copy of the original manuscript.

for line, word for word, and even letter for letter.[2]

Classic scholar and historian, Dr. Colin J. Hemer writes:

> With the Bible . . . you have impeccable history, which has been proven right in hundreds of details and never proven wrong, and it is written within one generation while eye-witnesses were still alive . . . [who] could have disputed it, if it were exaggerated or false.[3]

American archaeologist, philologist[4] and expert on ceramics, William F. Albright says:

> Critics of the New Testament are 'pre-archaeological' and their views are quite antiquated.[5]

There may be no more convincing proof of the reliability of the Bible than the manuscript evidence that is available. When you consider the New Testament manuscripts, you will be astounded by the sheer number of copies which are still in existence.

New Testament Manuscript Copies

A primary means of ascertaining the Bible's credibility is the number of ancient copies we have in our possession.[6] The more copies we have, the better we can compare them and know how well the Bible we now read corresponds with the original. It is much like having a witness to an event. If we have only one witness to the event, there

---

2 Geisler and Nix, 238.

3 Ibid.

4 Philology is the study of written records to determine their authenticity, original form, and meaning.

5 *Biblical Archaeology—Silencing the Critics*. John Ankerberg. www.jashow.org /articles/ general/biblical-archaeology—silencing-the-critics-part-2.

6 For a good resource on this topic see Dr. Charles A. Crane, *The Bible: The True and Reliable Word of God*.

---

remains the possibility that the witness' agenda, or even an exaggeration of the event, has crept in and we might not know the truth. But if we have many witnesses, we can compare testimonies and reach a verified conclusion about what really happened.

When it comes to New Testament manuscripts, we can have great assurance. There are over 5,600 Greek manuscripts; 10,000 Latin Vulgate manuscripts; 9,300 copies of other ancient works; and more which bear testimony to the accuracy of the Bible.[7] In addition, the manuscripts of the New Testament were written much closer to the original writings than any other work of ancient literature.[8] The closer the dates; the more reliable the data.

In addition to the nearly 25,000 manuscripts mentioned above, and due to the fact that Christianity was a missionary faith from its very inception, we have more than 15,000 copies in various other languages, including: Coptic translations (early 3rd and 4th centuries), Armenian translations (3rd century), Gothic translations (4th century), Georgian translations (5th century), Ethiopic translations (6th century), and Nubian translations (6th century). The fact that we have so many translations of the New Testament in various languages which all contain an identical message points to its authenticity.

Lectionaries[9] and Early Church Fathers

The practice of reading passages from the New Testament books at worship services began very early in church history. Various passages from the New Testament were recorded in lectionaries of which we have 2,135 copies that have been cataloged. A large portion of the

---

7 See Section Three (page 76) in *The Bible: The True and Reliable Word of God*, by Dr. Charles A. Crane. Endurance Press: 2014.

8 For more information on this, see *The Bible: The True and Reliable Word of God*.

9 A lectionary is a collection of scriptural readings from the Bible to be used in worship services at various times or occasions.

New Testament can be reproduced from these readings by which we can attest to the accuracy of our manuscripts. In addition, and possibly the greatest attestation for the accuracy of the New Testament, are the masses of quotations taken from the New Testament and quoted by the early church fathers. There are more than 32,000 quotations from the New Testament found in writings which date before the council of Nicea in A.D. 325.[10]

J. Harold Greenlee points out that biblical quotations found in the works of the early church writers are so extensive that the New Testament could virtually be reconstructed from them without using other New Testament manuscripts. Sir David Dalrymple put this statement to the test by using second and third century writings of the church fathers. He found all but eleven verses of the entire New Testament quoted within these writings.[11]

Some examples of the early church fathers who quote the New Testament include the writings of Clement (A.D. 30–95),[12] Ignatius (A.D. 70–110),[13] and Polycarp (A.D. 70–156).[14]

With all the many and varied sources, there is no evidence whatsoever which suggests that the Bible has been tampered with in any way or that the versions we now possess have been corrupted. In fact, with all this evidence, it is logically absurd to think that the early church tried to collect all extant copies scattered throughout the region, gather them up and burn the variant copies.

---

10 *Evidence that Demands a Verdict,* 1972, p. 51.

11 Ibid.

12 Clement quotes from various sections through out the New Testament.

13 Ignatius knew the Apostles personally and quotes from 15 of the 27 New Testament books.

14 Polycarp was a disciple of the Apostle John and quoted extensively from the New Testament.

Interestingly enough, there is no evidence that this has ever happened with our New Testament Scriptures, BUT this is exactly what happened in the case of Islam and the Qur'an. The third caliph, Uthman ibn Affan, ordered all copies to be gathered up and all variant versions of the Qur'an to be burned in A.D. 657.[15]

The Muslim claim that the New Testament has been corrupted is not only untrue, but its authenticity can be voluminously substantiated.

The Muslim Dilemma

Ironically, while modern-day Islam rejects the Bible as corrupt, the Qur'an itself commands Muslims to read the Gospels (*Injil*). Few Muslims are aware of this command.

> Say ye: "We believe in Allah, and the revelation given to us, and to Abraham, Isma'il, Isaac, Jacob, and the Tribes, and that given to Moses and Jesus, and that given to (all) prophets from their Lord: We make no difference between one and another of them" (Surah 2:136).

> If thou wert in doubt as to what We have revealed unto thee, then ask those who have been reading the Book (the Torah and the Gospel) from before thee: the Truth hath indeed come to thee from thy Lord: so be in no wise of those in doubt (Surah 10:94).

In so doing, Islam both rejects the Bible and requires the Bible. If Muslims accept what the Qur'an teaches, they must then accept what the Bible teaches—which rejects what the Qur'an teaches. That's the Muslim dilemma.

Muslims are told:

> Observe the Torah and the Gospels . . . what is revealed to them from Allah (Dawood, 384).

---

15 See Chapter Five in this work for further details.

Believe in God and His Messenger [Muhammed] and the Book
He has sent down on His Messenger [The Qur'an] and the Book
which He sent down before [The Bible]. Whoso disbelieves in
God and His angels and His Books, and His Messengers, and the
Last Day, has surely gone astray into fat error . . .[16]

This becomes a great place for witnessing as the Qur'an
instructs Muslims in the validity of the Bible and its message about
Jesus. In the Qur'an, Jesus is called "Muhammed's Lord" (Surah
89:22) and the Truth (Surah 2:91). The Qur'an also describes Jesus
as the "Word of God" (Surah 3:45; 4:171) and a "Spirit proceeding
forth from God" (Surah 4:171).

The Attractiveness of the Gospels

Give your Muslim friend one of the Gospels to read. This will point
them to who Jesus is, what he said, and what he did. The Gospel
of Mark or the Gospel of Luke would be a good place to start. The
Gospels will present Jesus to them and might create a thirst for more.

---

16 Arberry, *The Qur'an Interpreted*, 120-121.

Sixteen

Correctly Understanding the Crusades

For some time, the word "crusade" has been a highly charged term and many recently have accused the United States of being modern day "crusaders" against Islam. This view is wrong on so many different levels.

First, most people have the mistaken view that the Crusades were conducted by "evil war-mongering Christians" who fought against the "peace-loving" Muslims in Palestine throughout the Middle Ages.[1] This is exactly the opposite of the truth!

Second, some suggest that the actions of radical Islam as they cut off the heads of Christians are no different than the past actions of Christians during the Crusades. Characteristically, former President of the United States, Barack Obama, put forward the idea that during the Crusades, Christians committed "vast crimes against the world."[2]

---

1 Ridley Scott released a movie in 2005 called *The Kingdom of Heaven*, which also puts forward this erroneous idea that the Christians were the aggressors against secular Muslims who simply desired peaceful coexistence.

2 Former president Bill Clinton said, "In the first Crusade, when the Christian soldiers

This is at best hyperbole and at worst, an outright lie. What is often espoused as equivalent—the actions of jihadists and the actions of the Crusades—displays a blind eye to the long-term Muslim atrocities and the largely short-term military defense of the Crusades. Europe would have been overrun without a period of Crusades to defend Europe.

Unfortunately, the Crusades have been the target of revisionist history. One recent scholar has tried to correct the record when he wrote that "the crusades are quite possibly the most misunderstood event in European history."[3] In keeping with this point, I need to offer some harsh words of correction for those revisionists who have distorted (often intentionally) the history of the Middle Ages.

In what follows, do not hear me trying to justify the Crusades or the Crusaders, but I do want to put the events in their proper context. It is often taught that Western Christianity (Catholicism), driven by a religious fervor and dreams of personal profit, launched a religious campaign against Islam. The story line usually begins by saying that Christianity, as the aggressors, tried for 200 years to expel the Muslims from the Holy Land.

History, rather, shows that the Crusades began as a formal appeal for help. It clearly shows that Pope Urban II, in A.D. 1095, responded to an appeal for help from Alexius I. His motive in responding may have included his wish to pull the various factions of Catholicism back together again by uniting them behind a common cause in the first Crusade. What is often left out is that the Emperor

---

took Jerusalem, they . . . proceeded to kill every woman and child who was a Muslim on the temple mound . . . with blood running up to their knees. I can tell you that that story is still being told today in the Middle East and we are still paying for it." As quoted by Robert Louis Wiklen, "Rescuers, Not Invaders," *Wall Street Journal*, March 13, 2010.

3 Thomas F. Madden, "Crusade Propaganda: The Abuse of Christianity's Holy War," www.nationalreview.com (Aug 18, 2003).

needed reinforcements in his conflict with the westward-migrating Turks.

The Turks were Islamic tribes who were invading the often-Christian lands. Urban II responded to the appeal from Alexis I for help (he was the forward-looking Byzantine emperor from A.D. 1081 to 1118) and issued a decree for Christians to take up the cross. He is quoted as saying, "Wrest that land from the wicked race."

Most who teach about the Crusades treat it merely as a bloody affair launched by Christians, driven by their irrational religious bigotry and committing vast crimes against humanity. While it may be true that atrocities were committed during the Crusades, this revisionist retelling of history forgets the context in which the Crusades occurred.

Pope Urban II's decree did not take place in a vacuum.[4] It came at the request for reinforcements against the Muslim army. Here is Pope Urban II's plea for help:

> Your brethren who live in the east are in urgent need of your help, and you must hasten to give them the aid which has often been promised them. For, as most of you have heard, the Turks and Arabs have attacked them . . . and have overcome them in seven battles. They have killed and captured many, and have destroyed the churches and devastated the empire.[5]

Furthermore, it is necessary to remember that before the rise of Islam, the Middle East was predominantly Christian. Most of the people in what we now call Iraq, Syria, Jordan, and Egypt were Christians. The sacred places of Christianity—where Christ was born, lived, and died—are in that region. Inspired by Islam's call to jihad,

---

4 For more on this, see Joseph Michaud, *History of the Crusades*, vol 3, p 17-18.

5 As quoted by Katharine J. Lualdi, *Source of the Making of the West*, Volume I: To 1740: Peoples and Cultures, 196.

Muhammed and his armies conquered those areas. The instigator was not Pope Urban II, but Muhammed himself. And those who fought back during the Crusades were not just Christians, but also included the ruling dynasties who had previously been invaded.

Do any of these revisionist historians remember that it was Muhammed who initiated the first battles with the Battle of Badr (A.D. 624), the Battle of Uhud (625) and the Battle of the Trench (627)? Following Muhammed's death the battles continued with the invasion of Palestine (633), Yarmouk (626), Syria (627), Jerusalem (638), Egypt (641), Persia (642), the northern part of Africa (643), and Spain (711). Further invasions took place in the Battle of Tours in France (732).

Even after A.D. 732, the Islamic aggressions continued. Constantinople was attacked seven times between 668 and 798. The Islamic invasion spread throughout Europe and into Sicily (827) and into Rome itself (846). The Muslim invaders plundered churches and attacked Christians. These invasions continued in Spain into the 10th and the 11th centuries.

The numerous Islamic attacks and conquests continued for hundreds of years—long before the Crusades were launched in A.D. 1095. Unfortunately, these numerous attacks that precede the Crusades are not mentioned in school textbooks or noted in accounts that detail the history of the Crusades. Instead, there are scores of historians who lay the entire fault of the Crusades on the conscience of Christians. It has been a huge lie!

Who were the Crusaders? The Crusaders included Christians who followed the battle cry of the church, but also included the very people who had been displaced, who were fighting back for their countries, and who were fighting for the very survival of Europe. Truth be told, if it were not for the Crusades, many more countries would be speaking Arabic!

Now, it is true, there were episodes of great unworthiness committed during the Crusades. Contrary to the stated goal of the Crusades, and certainly contrary to the central tenet of Christianity, Crusaders often pillaged as they traveled, innocent people were killed, and other immoralities occurred. There were unthinkable atrocities that should not have happened—but these rampages do not define the Crusades as a whole. In the context of the history of warfare (and it was war), there is no warrant for considering the Crusades a crime of any sort. People (including Christians and non-Christians) fought to regain their land and heritage.

Let me say it again, some of what happened during the Crusades (as often happens with war in general) was inappropriate. But it is imperative for you to remember—those who committed these crimes were transgressing the bounds of Christianity. *Christianity never holds the sword as the way to extend Christ's church.*[6] What is also often left unsaid is that the Pope even excommunicated some Crusaders for their inappropriate acts of violence.

As for the Muslims who murder, rape, pillage, and enslave— they have violated no Islamic principles and are not condemned nor excommunicated by their religious leaders. They are actually following the example of their prophet Muhammed and the next four Islamic leaders who followed him. The sword is the mantra of Islam and Politically Correct lies obscure the nature of the long-term evil in the Islamic wars, justifying their killing, murder, slavery, rape, and territorial conquering of previously peaceful kingdoms.

---

6 For more on The Bible and Violence see Appendix D.

Conclusion: Part Two

According to Pew Research Center, 85,000 refugees entered the United States in 2016. Nearly 50% of those were known Muslim refugees. That number was up over 200% since the year 2002. Overall, the United States admitted 279,339 Muslim refugees between 2002 and 2016.

But that is only a fraction of the real story. Refugees make up only a small percentage (less than 10%) of the roughly one million immigrants who were granted lawful permanent residency in the United States each year. Because the United States government does not keep track of the religion of new legal immigrants, it is not possible to estimate what share of all recent immigrants are Muslim. But if the actual numbers of Muslim immigrants were only 10-20 percent of the total new immigrants to the United States, this would mean that an additional 100,000 to 200,000 Muslims are entering the United States each year.

This being the case, reaching Muslims for Christ should not simply be a global missions outreach—it should be our local missions outreach. In order to move forward as Christians, we must not only know about Islam (Part One of this book), we must be ready and equipped to reach our Muslim neighbors for Christ (Part Two of this book).

But we need to take one further step. In addition to reaching Muslims for Christ, we must also be willing to care for our Muslim neighbors who come to Christ.

Help for Muslim Converts to Christianity

Converts from Islam to Christianity generally face rejection or worse. In some Islamic cultures, it is not only illegal for a Muslim to convert, but the penalty is death. Obviously, this extreme penalty is not a major problem in the United States. Short of death, however, ostracization and animosity from family and friends is almost always the case—even in the United States. Rejection may include threats of violence, black-listing, or withdrawal of aid or financial support. A convert may be expelled from the home. A married convert will probably lose access (even if illegally) to their children or grandchildren. An employed convert in certain circumstances might possibly even lose their job if employed by a Muslim employer.

This being the case, the Church must become the convert's new family, and this means more than just saying hello after Sunday services. Real support and practical provisions may be necessary.

There will also be difficulty stemming from other areas. It is often difficult for a Muslim to adjust to the freedom we have in Christ. Islam is so regulated that a convert can be left feeling a sense of desperation about what to do and how to live. It is imperative to provide ongoing discipleship and accountability.

The question for all of us is simply this: will we demonstrate our love for Christ, not only by knowing about Islam, not simply by sharing Christ with Muslims, but by helping our Muslim neighbors as they transition their allegiance to THE PRINCE OF PEACE?

Nations Totally or Predominantly Muslim

Afghanistan—population 23 million, almost totally Muslim

Albania—seventy percent of its more than three million people are Muslim

Algeria—more than 29 million people, almost totally Muslim

Azerbaijan—almost eight million people, almost totally Muslim

Bahrain—600,000 people, 100% Muslim

Bangladesh—124 million inhabitants, 83% Muslim

Brunei—300,000 people, 67% Muslim

Burkina Faso—11 million people, 50% Muslim

Chad—two million, 50% Muslim

Comoros—600,000, 85% Muslim

Djibouti—430,000, 94% Muslim

Egypt—64 million, 94% Muslim

Gambia—one-and-a-half million, 90% Muslim

Guinea—seven-and-a-half million, 85% Muslim

Indonesia—207 million, 87% Muslim (largest number in the world)

Iran—66 million, almost totally Shiite Muslim

Iraq—21 million, almost totally Sunni Muslim

Ivory Coast—15 million, 60% Muslim

Jordan—four million, almost totally Sunni Muslim

Kazakstan—17 million, almost all Muslim

Kuwait—two million, almost all Muslim

Kyrgyzstan—five million, almost all Muslim

Lebanon—four million, 70% Muslim

Libya—six million, totally Sunni Muslim

Malaysia—20 million people, almost all Muslim

Maldives—275,000, all Muslim

Mali—275,000, all Muslim

Mauritania—three million, totally Muslim

Morocco—30 million, all Muslim

Niger—104 million, 50% Muslim

Nigeria—104 million, 50% Muslim

Oman—two million, entirely Muslim

Pakistan—130 million, entirely Muslim

Qatar—550,000, 95% Muslim

Saudi Arabia—19.5 million, all Muslim

Senegal—nine million, 92% Muslim

Sierra Leone—five million, 60% Muslim

Somalia—10 million, almost all Muslim

Sudan—31 million, 70% Muslim

Syria—15.6 million, 75% Muslim

Tajikistan—six million, 80% Muslim

Tunisia—nine-and-a-half million, 98% Muslim

Turkey—62 million, all Muslim

Turkmenistan—nine million, all Muslim

United Arab Emirates—three million, all Muslim

Uzbekistan—23 million, mostly Muslim

Western Sahara—entirely Muslim

Yemen—13 million, almost totally Muslim, but divided into three
sects

Other large populations: **Bosnia, Ghana, India, Israel, Singapore,**
the **Philippines, Trinidad.** Also increasing numbers in **Canada** and
the **United States** as well as **England.**

Appendix B

Chronological Order of the Qur'an

The following list presents the traditional Islamic chronological order of the surahs. There are some slight variations of the order depending upon the source used, but the division of Mecca and Medina surahs remains consistent.

As you look at the order of these surahs, remember the principle of abrogation.

Mecca Surahs

96, *68, *73, 74, 1, 111, 81, 87, 92, 89, 93, 94, 103, 100, 108, 102, *107, 109, 105, 113, 114, 112, *53, 80, 97, 91, 85, 95, 106, 101, 75, 104, *77, *50, 90, 86, *54, 38, *7, 72, *36, *25, 35, *19, *20, *56, *26, 27, *28, *17, *10, *11, *12, *15, *6, 37, *31, 34, 39, *40, 41, *42, *43, 44, *45, *46, 51, 88, *18, *16, 71, *14, 21, 23, *32, 52, 67, 69, 70, 78, 79, 82, 84, *30, *29, 83.

*Portions of these surahs contain verses ('ayats) that were later revealed in Medina.

Medina Surahs

2, 8, 3, 33, 60, 4, 99, 57, 47, 13, 55, 76, 65, 98, 59, 24, 22, 63, 58, 49, 66, 64, 61, 62, 48, 5, 9, 110.

Appendix C

Jihad in the Qur'an

Most scholars count over 100 jihad passages in the Qur'an. For the sake of brevity, this appendix quotes only about a fourth of these. It should also be noted that there are no Qur'anic verses that compare with that of "love your enemies, and pray for those who persecute you" (Matt 5:44) or, "If anyone slaps you on the right cheek, turn to him the other also" (Matt 5:39).

Fight in the cause of Allah those who fight you ... (Surah 2:190).

And slay them wherever ye catch them, and turn them out from where they have turned you out; for Persecution is worse than slaughter; but fight them not at the Sacred Mosque, unless they (first) fight you there; but if they fight you, slay them. Such is the reward of those who reject Faith (Surah 2:191).

And fight them on until there is no more Persecution and the religion becomes Allah's ... (Surah 2:193).

Fighting is prescribed upon you, and ye dislike it. But it is possible that ye dislike a thing which is good for you, and that ye love a thing which is bad for you. But Allah knoweth, and ye know not (Surah 2:216).

Then fight in the cause of Allah, and know that Allah heareth and knoweth all things (Surah 2:244).

Remember that morning though didst leave they household (early) to post the Faithful at their stations for battle: and Allah heareth and knoweth all things (Surah 3:121).

And if ye are slain, or die, in the way of Allah, forgiveness and mercy from Allah are far better than all they could amass (Surah 3:157).

And if ye die, or are slain, lo! it is unto Allah that ye are brought together (Surah 3:158).

Let those fight in the cause of Allah who sell the life of this world for the Hereafter. To him who fighteth in the cause of Allah,—whether he is slain or gets victory—soon shall We give him a reward of great (value) (Surah 4:74).

Those who believe fight in the cause of Allah, and those who reject Faith fight in the cause of Evil (*Tagut*): so fight ye against the friends, of Satan: feeble indeed is the cunning of Satan (Surah 4:76).

Then fight in Allah's cause—thou art held responsible only for Thyself—and rouse the Believers. It may be that Allah will restrain the fury of the Unbelievers; for Allah is the strongest in might and in punishment (Surah 4:84).

They but wish that ye should reject Faith, as they do, and thus be on the same footing (as they): so take not friends from their ranks until they flee in the way of Allah (from what is forbidden). But if they turn renegades, seize them and slay them wherever ye find them; and (in any case) take no friends or helpers from their ranks (Surah 4:89).

Seize them and slay them wherever ye get them: in their case We have provided you with a clear argument against them (Surah 4:91).

The punishment of those who wage war against Allah and His Messenger, and strive with might and main for mischief through the land is: execution, or crucifixion, or the cutting off of hands and feet from opposite sides, or exile from the land: that is their disgrace in this world, and a heavy punishment is theirs in the

Hereafter (Surah 5:33).

Remember thy Lord inspired the angels (with the message): "I am with you: give firmness to the Believers: I will instil [sic] terror into the hearts of the Unbelievers: smite ye above their necks and smite all their finger-tips off them" (Surah 8:12).

O ye who believe! when ye meet the Unbelievers in hostile array, never turn your backs to them. If any do turn his back to them on such a day—unless it be in a stratagem of war, or to retreat to a troop (of his own)—he draws on himself the wrath of Allah, and his abode is Hell,—an evil refuge (indeed)! (Surah 8:15).

It is not ye who slew them; it was Allah . . . (Surah 8:17).

And fight them on until there is no more persecution, and religion becomes Allah's in its entirety . . . (Surah 8:39).

O Prophet! rouse the Believers to the fight. If there are twenty amongst you, patient and persevering, they will vanquish two hundred: if a hundred. They will vanquish a thousand of the Unbelievers: for these are a people without understanding (Surah 8:65).

But when the forbidden months are past, then fight and slay the Pagans wherever ye find them, and seize them, beleaguer them, and lie in wait form them in every stratagem (of war); but if they repent, and establish regular prayers and pay Zakat then open the way for them: For Allah is Oft-Forgiving, Most Merciful (Surah 9:5).

But if they violate their oaths after their covenant, and attack your Faith,—fight ye the chiefs of Unfaith: for their oaths are nothing to them: that thus they may be restrained (Surah 9:12).

Fight them, and Allah will punish them by your hands, and disgrace them help you (to victory) over them, heal the breasts of

Believers (Surah 9:14).

Fight those who believe not in Allah nor the Last Day, nor hold that forbidden which hath been forbidden by Allah and His Messenger, nor acknowledge the Religion of Truth, from among the People of the Book, until they pray the Jizya with willing submission, and feel themselves subdued (Surah 9:29).

O ye who believe! Fight the Unbelievers who are near to you and let them find harshness in you: and know that Allah is with those who fear him (Surah 9:123).

Therefore, when ye meet the Unbelievers (in fight), smite at their necks; at length, when ye have thoroughly subdued them, bind (the captives) firmly: therefore (is the time for) either generosity or ransom: until the war lays down its burdens. Thus (are ye commanded): but if it had been Allah's Will, he could certainly have exacted retribution from them (Himself); but (He lets you fight) in order to test you, some with others. But those who are slain in the way of Allah,—he will never let their deeds be lost (Surah 47:4).

Say to the desert Arabs who lagged behind: 'Ye shall be summoned (to fight) against a people given to vehement war: then shall ye fight, or they shall submit. Then if ye show obedience, Allah will grant you a goodly reward, but if ye turn back as ye did before, He will punish you with a grievous Chastisement (Surah 48:16).

Truly Allah loves those who fight in His Cause in battle array, as if they were a solid cemented structure (Surah 61:4).

O Prophet! Strive hard against the Unbelievers and the Hypocrites, and be harsh with them. Their abode is Hell,—an evil refuge (indeed) (Surah 66:9).

Appendix D

The Bible and Violence

W hen confronted with the violent nature of Islam, Muslims often are quick to reply that the Bible has violent passages also. This is a flawed response for two reasons.

The New Testament

While the Old Testament does have violent passages, including some that advocate violence against Israel's enemies, the New Testament has none. There is not a single verse in the entire New Testament that advocates violence. Instead, Jesus said, "If anyone slaps you on the right cheek, turn to him the other also" (Matthew 5:39).

In the early days of Christianity, when Christians were persecuted, there is no evidence that any of them engaged in any form of violence—not even in self-defense. Read the stories of the early church and the early Christian martyrs and you will not see war-like tendencies.

Later in history, as some acts of violence were carried out in the name of Christ, the people who engaged in that behavior did not have a single verse in the entire New Testament to support their violent acts.

The Old Testament

There is a further distinction when it comes to the violence found in the Old Testament. Unlike Muhammed, who called himself a prophet and used the sword to kill people, not one of the Old Testament prophets ever advocated using the sword, much less wield one. This is true of Isaiah, Jeremiah, Ezekiel, Daniel, Hosea, Joel, Amos, Obediah,

Jonah, Micah, Nahum, Habakkuk, Zephaniah, Haggai, Zechariah, Malachi, and all the other Hebrew prophets.

All the violent commands found in the Old Testament were directed to physical enemies of Israel with a specific purpose, and all those commands remain in Israel's past history. Neither Christians nor Jews use the violent passages of the Old Testament to promote or justify violence or killing people today. Period.

Appendix E

The Inaccurate Elevation of the Achievements of Islam

Islam has embarked on the deliberate process of disseminating false facts as history. Here a just a few examples which have no basis in fact or which have been grossly exaggerated in an attempt to make Islam look more attractive to an unsuspecting audience.

Arabic Numbers—that Islam invented our numeric system. The numerals 1, 2, 3, 4, etc., came to the West by way of the Arabs, but were originally derived from the Syriac alphabet and a Syrian mathematician. The idea of using zero in conjunction with those numerals came from India. During the ninth century, Arabs resisted accepting this new number set calling them "Indian numerals of the Hindus." Ironically, it is this very same number set that is now known as Arabic numerals.

Exploration and Conquest—that Napoleon Bonaparte converted to Islam; that Muslim explorers reached America before Christopher Columbus; that Islam discovered Australia. None of these have any historical merit.

Hospitals—that Islam is responsible for the first hospital(s). It is often claimed that the first hospital was founded in Baghdad under a ruling caliphate. It is true that a hospital was founded in the mid-700s in Baghdad. This hospital, however, was neither the first, nor it was not started by a Muslim. This hospital was founded by a Christian doctor named Jabrail ibn Bakhishu. Long before this time, during the first three centuries of Christianity's existence, "hospices" were established in an effort to follow Christ's commands to care for the sick and the physically needy. Building on the early hospice models, the first official "hospital" was built by St. Basil in Caesarea in Cappadocia in A.D. 369. A second hospital was built by a wealthy widow named Fabiola. She was an associate of Jerome who built a hospital in Rome in A.D. 390 and then another in Ostia in A.D. 398. The expansion of hospitals continued and multiplied in the fourth and fifth centuries. In the sixth century, hospitals became a common component of monasteries. The building of hospitals was a standard practice hundreds of years before ever reaching Baghdad.

Muslim Architecture—that Islam is responsible for architecture typical of mosques. The first mosques were actually Christian churches which had been captured. For example, Saint Sophia's in Turkey was built in A.D. 537 and served as an Eastern Orthodox church. The building was not converted into a mosque until May 29, 1453. The famous Dome of the Rock in Jerusalem was initially built in A.D. 691 and was patterned after nearby Byzantine churches that date back to A.D. 451. The minarets of mosques were also a copy of the stand-alone bell towers of early churches.

Science and Medicine—that Islam is responsible for the first medical books, the first philosophy books, and great advancements in mathematics, astronomy, zoology, chemistry, and geography. While there was much material that was written down in Arabic, many of the scholars were actually Christians and Jews. Other material was simply the translation of earlier Greek material into Arabic with little or nothing new in terms of advancement. What medieval Islam did well was to adapt the learning of other cultures and rename things in Arabic vernacular.

Alvin J. Schmidt writes:

> It is well to remember that Muslims discovered no scientific laws, such as Kepler's three laws in astronomy, Newton's law of gravity, Pascal's law of liquid pressure, Ohm's law in the field of electricity, Boyle's law in chemistry, Kelvin's absolute zero, Faraday's electromagnetic induction, Dalton's atomic weights, Lavoisier's law of the conservation of energy, or Mendel's law pertaining to heredity. Nor did any Muslims discover bacteria, introduce chloroform, inoculate against diseases, discover circulation of the blood, introduce antiseptics, or encourage the dissecting of human cadavers. These and other great moments in science were by-products of Christianity's influence, all outside the context of any Islamic influence or motivation. Hence ... the myth that Islam has encouraged science.[1]

---

1 *The Great Divide: The Failure of Islam and the Triumph of the West*, p. 200.

Appendix F

Glossary of Terms

Abrogate: To repeal or cancel by authority. In Islam, later revelation abrogates former revelation, and Sharia law abrogates all human regulation.

Abulations: Washing of the body, especially as part of a religious ceremony.

Adhan: The Muslim call to prayer called out five times a day.

Ahl-al-kitab: People of the book (Jews and Christians).

Alhamdolillah: "All praise be to Allah." This is the equivalent to hallelujah.

Allah: Arabic word for God. Specifically used by Muslims as the God of Islam.

Aqeedah: Deeply help Islamic beliefs.

Arkan-ud-din: The pillars of religion.

Al-Qaeda: The fundamentalist terrorist network formerly led by Osama bin Laden.

Ayah: Literally "sign." It is a verse of the Qur'an.

Azan or Adhan: The daily call to prayer by the muezzins.

Bismillah: In the name of Allah.

Burqa: Clothing that covers a woman in public, covering her whole body.

Caliph or Khalif: Title of the spiritual and political leaders who followed Muhammed.

Caliphate: A political-religious state under Sharia law.

Dawah: Inviting people to Islam. Literally, call or invitation.

Dhikr: Devotional acts in which the worshiper tries to be absorbed into oneness with Allah by chanting short phrases or prayers repeatedly.

Dhimmi: A non-Muslim in an Islamic society. These are to be subjugated people who are treated as second-class citizens.

Din: Religion as it is put into practice.

Doctrine of Abrogation: The teaching that verses or doctrine have been repealed or replaced by later revelation or that certain teachings take precedent over others in certain circumstances.

Du'aa: Specific Muslim prayers recited at certain occasions which may be improvised as opposed to ritual prayer called salaat.

Eid al-Fitr: One of two major Muslim holidays. This marks the end of Ramadan.

Fajr: The prayer at dawn.

Fatiha: The first surah in the Qur'an.

Fatwa: A ruling decision by a Muslim authority.

Five Pillars of Islam: Chief duties of Muslims: recite the creed, pray, fast, give alms, make a pilgrimage.

Gaza Strip: The area in Southwestern Israel along the Mediterranean Sea which is occupied by Palestinians.

Ghusl: Bathing the entire body.

Hadith (plural Ahadith): A story; an oral tradition later written down of what Muhammed said or approved of. Most often quoted as recorded in a sets of six books called the Sahih Sittah.

Hafiz: A man who has memorized the entire Qur'an.

Hajj: Pilgrimage to Mecca.

Hajji: Also Hadji. One who has made the pilgrimage to Mecca.

Halal: Arabic for permissible. Halal food is that which adheres to Islamic law, as defined by the Qur'an. The Islamic form of slaughtering animals involves the cutting of the jugular vein, carotid artery and windpipe, along with the pronouncement of the correct Islamic prayer.

Hamas: Terrorist group centered in Israel and adjacent regions.

Hezbollah (or Hizbollah): Terrorist group centered in Lebanon.

Hijab: A woman's veil or head scarf. Literally, it means partition or curtain.

Hijra: Muhammed's flight from Mecca to Medina in A.D. 622, the date used by Muslims to divide all time and begin the Muslim era.

Hudud: Fixed punishments for certain crimes as specified in the Qur'an. Examples include amputation for theft, flogging for drinking alcohol.

Ibadat: Unchangeable Sharia rules regarding worship and ritual.

Iblis: One of the names for the Devil or Satan.

Iftar: The meal eaten after fasting during Ramadan.

Ijma: A decision, once determined that is forced into law. Determined by consensus of Islamic scholars.

Imam: A spiritual leader looked upon by Shiite Muslims as a legitimate decendent of Muhammed and an authority on spiritual matters.

Infidel: One who rejects the teaching of Islam.

Injil: The gospels as originally given (Good News).

Inshallah: "If Allah wills it."

Isa: Arabic word for Jesus.

Isah: The night prayer or fifth prayer.

Ishmael: First son of Abraham through his wife's maid. Muslims believe that the promise of God came through Ishmael, not Isaac.

ISIL: Islamic State of Iraq and the Levant. Levant refers to a region of Middle Eastern countries along the eastern border of the Mediterranean Sea including: Cyprus, Israel, Jordan, Lebanon, Syria and Turkey.

ISIS: Islamic State of Iraq and Syria. Islamic group which has laid siege to parts of Syria and Iraq. Their stated goal is to restore a caliphate.

Isnad: The chain of transmission for a hadith.

Islamic Jihad: Fundamentalist terrorist group centered in Egypt.

Janna: Literally a garden. The term used for paradise.

Jihad: Literally, an effort of striving. Sacred struggle or holy war.

Jilbab: Full-length outer garment for Muslim women.

Jinn: An evil spirit.

Jizyah: Tax that must be paid by anyone who chooses to keep their own faith and not convert to Islam.

Jumaa: The Muslim holy day which occurs on Friday.

Ka'ba or Kaaba: A cubicle stone in the court of the mosque in Mecca toward which Muslims pray. They touch or kiss the sacred stone which they believe was built by Abraham.

Kafir: Infidel, non-Muslim.

Kalima: Islamic creed.

Khadija: Muhammed's first wife who was wealthy. She convinced him that God was talking to him.

Khalifa: The supreme leader over Islam. Usually the title is used to refer to one of Muhammed's four successors.

Khutba: The sermon given on the Muslim holy day.

Kibla: A niche in Mosques and homes which point to Mecca.

Kismat: It is my lot (an expression of fatalism).

Maghrib: The sunset or evening prayer. The fourth prayer.

Mahdi: The coming Messiah of Islam. Many Muslims believe that by ushering war they can hasten the appearance of the Mahdi.

Maktub: It is written (an expression of fatalism).

Maqdur: It is decided (an expression of fatalism).

Masjid: The Muslim place of worship often called a mosque.

Mecca: City in Saudi Arabia; the birthplace of Muhammed, considered the most holy city of Islam.

Medina: The second-most holy city of Islam. Located to the north of Mecca. Muhammed's grave is located in the Holy Mosque of the Prophet.

Mihrab: A niche in the wall of a mosque which indicates the direction of prayer towards Mecca.

Miraj: The miraculous night journey of Muhammed to heaven.

Minaret: Tower of a mosque from which the call to prayer is made.

Mizan: The scales on which good and bad deeds are weighed.

Mosque: A Muslim place of worship.

Muhammed: Founder of Islam. Considered to be a messenger from God and the last prophet. His full name is Muhammed Bin-Abdullah.

Mufti: A Muslim legal expert.

Muhammed: Founder of Islam, born in Mecca around A.D. 570 and died there in A.D. 632.

Muazzin or Muezzins: the mosque official who calls the faithful to prayer.

Muslim Brotherhood: Islamic organization encompassing several nations and Islamic groups.

Mujahed: One who goes to on jihad. An Islamic warrior.

Mullah: A religious teacher.

Nafl: Optional prayers seeking the help of Allah.

Naskh: System of interpreting the Qur'an where new verses override previous verses. Often called abrogation.

People of the Book: The name given by the Qur'an to Jews and Christians.

Qibia or Qiblah: The direction toward Mecca to be facing during prayer.

Qur'an: The Holy Scriptures of Islam. Given to Muhammed over a period of 23 years. Thought to be the perfect replica of the original in heaven.

Rakaat: Units of repetition in salaat accompanied by the various prayer postures.

Ramadan: Ninth month of the Islamic calendar, devoted to fasting in celebration of the Qur'an's first being revealed to humanity.

Rasul: An apostle.

Sahih Bukhari: The most trustworthy collection of hadith.

Sahih Sittah: The six books of hadith consider the most authentic which includes Sahih Bukhari.

Salaat: Ritual prayer, primarily the five daily prayers.

Saum or Sawm: Fasting during the month of Ramadan.

Schri: The meal eaten before fasting.

Shahadah: Recitation of the Muslim creed.

Sharia: Muslim religious law meaning "the path."

Sheikh: Term of reverence for an ordained religious leader in Islam.

Shiites: A major Islamic sect that traces belief through Muhammed's son-in-law.

Shirk: Association of any other being with Allah. The worst sin in Islam.

Sirah: Biographies of Muhammed's life.

Sirat: The hair-narrow bridge which every person must cross to enter paradise.

Six Articles of Faith: The fundamental beliefs of Islam.

Sufis: A mystical sect of Islam that renounces the world.

Sunnah: Custom, a way of acting, written tradition. Recorded life of Muhammed.

Sunni: A major sect of Islam which follows the four caliphs (Abu Bakr, 'Umar, 'Uthman, and 'Ali).

Surah (or Sura): A chapter in the Qur'an.

Takfir: The act of declaring that another Muslim is not a genuine believer but an infidel.

Talaq: A word used by a husband to divorce his wife.

Taliban: Islamic fundamentalist group of Afghanistan.

Taqiya: Dissimulation. The practice of lying and deceiving for the purpose of advancing the cause of Islam.

Taraweeh: Voluntary prayers offered at night during Ramadan.

Tariqa: Meditation.

Tauheed or Tawhid: The Islamic doctrine of Allah's absolute unity and sovereignty.

Ulema: Principles Muslim scholars reach by consensus.

Ummah: Family, community, tribe.

Wahhabi: Sect within the Sunni branch of Islam that preaches a strict intolerant version of Islam.

West Bank: Land in Israel west of the Jordan River, most of which is occupied by Palestinians and is a source of much conflict.

Wudhu: Ceremonial washing before prayer (salaat). It is necessary to wash those parts of the body which are generally exposed.

Yam al-akhirah: The day of judgment.

Zakat: Mandatory giving.

Zakah or Zakat: A religious offering or tax on all of one's possessions. This is not voluntary, but forced. It is distributed only to those who are said to be entitled to receive it. It has been the avenue by which many Jihad activities have been financed and Islamic terrorists funded.

Zabur: The Psalms.

Ziyara: A visit to Muhammed's tomb in Medina. Often used of the tomb of any Muslim holy person.

Zuhr: The mid-day prayer. Second prayer.

Bibliography

Abdul-Haqq, Abdiyah Akbar. *Sharing Your Faith with a Muslim.* Minneapolis: Bethany Fellowship, Inc., 1980.

Ahmed, Akbar. *Islam Today.* London: I.B. Tauris, 1999.

Al Araby, Abdulla. *Islam Unveiled.* 8th ed. Los Angeles: The Pen vs. the Sword, 2001.

Ankerberg, John and John Weldon. *Fast Facts on Islam: What You Need to Know Now.* Eugene: Harvest House, 2001.

Beverly, James A. *Christ and Islam: Understanding the Faith of the Muslims.* Joplin, MO: College Press, 1997.

_____. *"Islam a Religion of Peace?"* Christianity Today, 46, No. 1 (Jan 7, 2002).

Bickel, Bruce and Stan Jantz. *Bruce and Stan's Pocket Guide to Islam.* Eugene: Harvest House, 2002.

Caner, Ergum Mehmet and Emir Fethi Caner. *Unveiling Islam: An Insider's Look at Muslim Life and Belief.* Grand Rapids: Kregel, 2002.

Cook, David. *Understanding Jihad.* Berkeley: University of California, 2005.

Crane, Charles A. *The Bible: The True and Reliable Word of God.* Endurance Press: Star, ID, 2014.

Federer, William J. *What Every American Needs to Know About the Qur'an.* Amerisearch, 2016.

Gabriel, Mark A. *Islam and Terrorism.* Lake Mary, Florida: Charisma House, 2002.

Geisler, Norman L, and Abdul Saleeb. *Answering Islam.* Grand Rapids: Baker, 1993.

Cragg, Kenneth. *The Call of the Minaret.* NY: Oxford University Press, 1964.

_____. *Jesus and the Muslim*, London: George Allen and Unwin, 1985.

Gibbon, Edward. *The History of the Decline and Fall of the Roman Empire*. Taylor & Francis, 1997.

Ghyselinck, Richard. *Islam: An Overview*. Eau Clair Printing, 2015.

Hirsi Ali, Ayaan. *Heretic: Why Islam Needs a Reformation Now*. NY: HarperCollins Publishers, 2015.

Lippman, Thomas. *Understanding Islam*. New York: Penguin Books, 1990.

Masih, Abd-Al. *Who Is Allah in Islam?*, Austria: Light of Life, 1985.

Qureshi, Nabeel. *No God But One: Allah or Jesus?* Zondervan: 2016.

_____. *Seeking Allah. Finding Jesus: A Devout Muslim Encounters Christianity*. Zondervan: 2014.

Saal, William J. *Reaching Muslims for Christ*. Chicago: Moody Press, 1991.

Schmidt, Alvin J. *The Great Divide: The Failure of Islam and the Triumph of the West*. Boston: Regina Orthodox Press Inc, 2004.

Spencer, Robert. *Islam Unveiled: Disturbing Questions about the World's Fastest-Growing Faith*. San Francisco: Encounter Books, 2002.

Steer, Malcolm. *A Christian's Evangelistic Pocket Guide to Islam*. Great Britain: Christian Focus Publications, 2004.

Shipp, Glover. *Christianity and Islam*. Webb City, MS: Covenant, 2002.

Shorrosh, A. *Islam Revealed*. Nashville, TN: Thomas Nelson, 1988.

Sookhdeo, Patrick. *A Christian's Pocket Guide to Islam*. Great Britain: Cox and Wyman, 2001.

_____. *Dawa: The Islamic Strategy for Reshaping the Modern World*. Virginia: Isaac Publishing, 2014.

_____. *Islam and Truth*. Barnabas Fund, 2007.

_____. *Is the Muslim Isa the Biblical Jesus?* Barnabas Fund, 2012.

_____. *What is Islam?* Barnabas Fund, 2014.

_____. *What is Sharia?* Barnabas Fund, 2014.

Sumrall, Lester. *Jihad: The Holy War.* Tulsal: Harrison House, 1981.

Youssef, Michael. *Jesus, Jihad and Peace: What Bible Prophecy Says About World Events Today.* Worthy Books, 2015.

Warner, Bill. *Sharia Law for the Non-Muslim.* Center for the Study of Political Islam, 2010.

Youssef, Michael. *Blindsided: The Radical Islamic Conquest.* Kobri: self-published, 2012.

Qur'ans Cited

Maulana Muhammed Ali, *The Holy Qur'an: Arabic Text, English Translation and Commentary.* Columbus, OH: Ahmadiyyah Anjuman Ish'at Islam, 1996.

A. Yusuf Ali, *The Holy Qur'an.* Washington D.C.: The Islamic Center, 1978.

A.J. Arberry, *The Qur'an Interpreted.* NY: Macmillan, 1976.

N.J. Dawood, *The Qur'an.* Baltimore: Penguin Books, 1972.

J.M. Rodwell, *The Koran.* NY: Dutton, 1977.

Web Sites

www.answering-islam.org

www.persecution.com

Other Books by Dr. Steven A. Crane

Ashamed of Joseph, Mormon Foundations Crumble.
180 pages, $16.95. A biography of the Mormon Prophet Joseph Smith from a Christian point of view.

Is Mormonism Now Christian?
159 pages, $16.95. A fresh look at the distinctions between Evangelical Christianity and Mormonism to determine if the doctrinal distance between these two groups is shrinking.

Email Messages: A Minister Responds to Questions from His Congregation.
177 pages, $16.95. Answers given to often asked questions about Christianity.

Marveling with Mark: An Expository Commentary on the Second Gospel.
300 pages, $29.95. A systematic treatment of the Gospel of Mark with aids to understanding and communicating its message to a modern audience.

These books can be ordered from
Steven Crane
Eagle Christian Church
100 S. Short Rd
Eagle, ID 83616
Add $3.00 for mailing in the USA.
Larger quantity discounts available.

CPSIA information can be obtained
at www.ICGtesting.com
Printed in the USA
FSOW03n0804210517
34500FS